UNDAUNTED
SPIRITS

UNDAUNTED SPIRITS

Portraits of Recovery from Trauma

by

Mary Baures

The Charles Press, Publishers

Philadelphia

The Charles Press, Publishers
Post Office Box 15715
Philadelphia, PA 19103
(215) 545-8933

Library of Congress Cataloging-in-Publication Data

Baures, Mary.
    Undaunted spirits: portraits of recovery from trauma / Mary Baures.
        p.   cm.
    ISBN 0-914783-71-8
    1. Stress (Psychology) — Case studies. 2. Resilience (Personality trait) — Case studies. 3. Adjustment (Psychology) — Case studies.
    4. Psychic trauma — Case studies. I. Title.
    RC 455.4.S87B38   1994
    155.8'042 — dc20   93-37931
                                                                            CIP

Printed in the United States of America

ISBN 0-914783-71-8

For my parents,
Robert A. Baures and
Ruth S. Baures

In every life there are experiences, painful and at first disorienting, which by their very intensity throw a sudden floodlight on the ways we have been living, the forces that control our lives.... Some people allow such illuminations only the brevity of a flash of sheet-lightening that throws a whole landscape into sharp relief, after which the darkness of denial closes in again. For others, these clarifications provide a motive and impulse toward a more enduring lucidity, a search for greater honesty, and for the recognition of larger issues of which our personal suffering is a symptom....

Adrienne Rich — *On Lies, Secrets and Silence*

Foreword

by Bernie Siegel, MD

Mary Baures' book is a pleasure to read. It is not only because of the wonderful lessons that can be learned from the survivors she interviews, but also because of the sense you will have that you are actually sitting with them, as she did. At times I felt so drawn into the story that I had to work to pay attention to the individual gems of thought that were being imparted. This book is so full of passion and feeling. And all of those interviewed have learned how to use this passion to heal not only themselves, but others as well.

The people Baures writes about are all winners, not because they conquered adverse circumstances and afflictions, but because they let the trauma open them to a new reality and a new understanding of healing that in turn allowed them to reach greater heights than they had reached before. Each of them make clear that healing and health are of the mind, not of the body. They teach us about becoming what Ernest Hemingway referred to as "strong at the broken places" and of the potential value of being wounded. As Thornton Wilder wrote, "In love's service only the wounded soldiers can serve."

Each story alone would be teacher enough, but to have them all together is especially powerful. The book helps us to look at the universal meaning of life and at the personal question of Why me? Life's rules, without exception, apply to everyone. It is painful, difficult and full of problems, but it is fair. This book shows how some people have dealt (or are still dealing) with life's difficulties in such an inspirational way that will help those of you who are also dealing with trauma.Those in this book tell us that they know that they cannot take illness, accidents and death out of life, so they invest their energy in what they know they can change.

Reading of the two participants who smoked cigarettes during their interviews with Mary made me think, "If life is so beautiful, why do they smoke?" People do things such as smoking because they are human, and because they are still working on themselves and their lives. Self-forgiveness is an important message shared by all of those interviewed.

These individuals serve as role models, and although it may seem at first like their resilience and perseverance is beyond your ability, they will inspire you to struggle courageously, even when life seems to be at its hardest. These remarkable people will help you to realize that you are every bit as capable of doing what they have done.

Accept the challenge of life, be a pupil and a teacher, and most of all, let these stories remind you of what William Saroyan said, "In the time of your life, live."

Acknowledgments

Many people contributed to the richness of this book. My professors at Harvard—Carol Gilligan, Howard Gardner and Robert Kegan—taught me about the human struggle toward development, and their visions became the theoretical underpinnings of this project.

Many professors from Antioch-New England contributed support, feedback and encouragement. I would also like to thank Dusty Miller, Phil Kinsler, David Singer and Susan Hawes.

I wish to acknowledge those survivors whose stories I collected, but was unable to include in this volume: Larry Howard, director of the J.F.K. Assassination Center in Dallas; Vietnam veteran Roger Helle, director of Teen Challenge of the Midlands; Jean Anne McLaughlin, actress and playwright; and documentary filmmaker David Sutherland.

I am also indebted to Kris Arriaga who translated during my interview with Armando Valladares.

I would like to give tribute to the late Joanne Carr, former Professor of Special Education at Suffolk University. Her belief in the human spirit's ability to overcome trauma and her frequent expression of this belief during our long friendship seeded some of my first ideas for this book.

I am grateful to those friends who provided comic relief during the writing process: William Newman, Andrea Zeren, Gila Lindsley, Clair Dion, Dianne Benedict,

Charlotte Hastings, Dale Conway, Deb Piper, Kate Cul-
hane, Vilot Morin, Roberta Feather, Britt Pearlman, Sue
Brower, Donna Whipple, Dave Terjanian and Al
Sciarappa.

   I appreciate the patience and attention to detail that
my editor, Lauren Meltzer, provided. I also would like to
thank Daryl Freeman, Chris Keane and Susan Crawford
for their editorial help. Thanks also to Nancy Sutherland
who helped me find participants to interview.

   Charles Figley, founder of the *Journal of Traumatic
Stress,* encouraged my research, as did Thomas Green-
ing, editor of the *Journal of Humanistic Psychology.* I
would also like to thank *New Hampshire Profiles* for
publishing a version of the interview with Nackey Loeb.

   Finally, I would like to thank Dr. Austin Kutscher,
President of The American Institute of Life-Threatening
Illness and Loss at Columbia-Presbyterian Medical Cen-
ter, who brought my manuscript to the attention of The
Charles Press and to Lawrence Meltzer, MD, who made
the decision to publish it.

                                                   M.B.

Contents

Introduction

For more than four years I worked on a psychiatric emergency team and I saw many people after they had attempted suicide. They said they had tried to kill themselves for reasons that seemed temporary and relatively minor: they had, for example, broken up with their boyfriend, lost their job, or had been evicted from their apartment. Although to me, most of their problems seemed more like setbacks, *they* saw them as overwhelming catastrophes. One problem made their whole existence seem so bleak that they did not want to live. The negative opinions they had about themselves and the world they lived in created more pain than they could bear. Some of these people were suicidal because they had no sustaining meanings by which to live: they were too poisoned by bitterness to invest in hopeful images of the future; they were impatient with the meager rewards from energetic or courageous efforts they may have attempted; and sometimes threats to their survival and integrity had gone on so long that their courage had been undermined by the dread that had become their world. For them, life could not be accepted on the terms for which it could be obtained.

Later, when I became involved in the management of catastrophe, I began to study people who had successfully survived extreme trauma. Those who survive severe trauma are not as well-known to clinicians as those who have been overwhelmed by severe catastrophe. Many of those who are defeated by a catastrophe have predictable psychological problems and are rendered helpless by forces that are often beyond their control. A severe trauma cannot leave a person's psyche unchanged. Some deaden parts of themselves to seal off the emotional wounds or feel overpowered and threatened, wondering if they will ever be able to return to life as they once knew it. Sometimes, in extreme cases, the mind can become distorted with terror, causing everything to seem full of danger and doom. Aspects of life that were once integrated become severed. Also, intense emotions can erupt, and the person has no memory of what is causing the feelings, or remembers the traumatic details, but not the memories that accompany them. For some, a catastrophe can become the object of such extreme obsession that the pain becomes the central focus of their life. Chronic stimulation of the nervous system can lead to profound and lasting changes in thinking, emotions and memory. It is, therefore, not hard to see why many people crumble under the stress of a catastrophe.

Compare the defeated with the survivors — people who have something crushing happen to them that assaults both body and spirit — but who, refusing to accept defeat, enter into a dynamic struggle to survive and find meaning in their loss. Those who can move on after a crisis discover that deep healing connects them to their greatest potential, to more authentic relationships and ultimately, to something more profound than their own selves. Despite the heat, oppression and intensity of the catastrophe, their psyches are stirred toward transcendence. As they regenerate and reconstruct, they become more porous and permeable and this gives them a greater connection to others, as well as more vitality and integrity than they had before the catastrophe. In addition, by repositioning their thoughts to a higher place, they can contemplate existence from a more universal point of view, and this also allows for growth and transformation. In stark contrast to the defeated, survivors are transformed by the adversity they encountered, like the phoenix, the mythical bird that is a universal symbol of resurrection, triumph, immortality and inseparable fellowship, who, after dying, is reborn, rising magnificently from the ashes that are the burnt remains of his old self.

How do some emotionally survive catastrophes while others become bitter, jaded and less of a person than they were previously? And who are the people who have managed to fight back, conquering their battles to emerge as better people? To answer these questions, I interviewed many survivors of severe trauma. Sixteen of the interviews and the stories they engendered became the basis of this book.

These stories can be seen as a blueprint of survivorship from extreme loss that will help others who, after a catastrophe, are struggling to find the inner strength and inspiration they need to keep going when life doesn't seem worth living any more.

After the ground beneath them caved in, all of the survivors I interviewed had to fight hard against being submerged by severe losses — traumas that robbed them of something central to who they were, something fundamental to their very being. When all previous methods of coping failed them, they too reached rock bottom, just like those I met in the emergency ward who had attempted to end their lives. But, instead of trying to run away, the survivors took a very different attitude toward the new and painful situations they were suddenly in. They were able to achieve something special; in the grip of despair, they reached above and beyond anything they had known before and fought back. They chose to explore the new problems they now had to contend with and began to ask some very profound questions about life and their place in it: "Who am I now? What is really important in life? How do I fit into the whole scheme of things? What is my connection to others?" The exceptional ability to seek something meaningful in dire situations, to discover a purpose in their crisis, enabled them to reposition themselves and embrace something more than their own suffering. In essence, by facing the threat of destruction and sometimes their own extinction, they learned that they had to align themselves with a force larger than themselves. (This concept is described further in the Afterword.) Alcoholics Anonymous and many other 12-step programs are based in large part on some of the same methods used, not only to stay afloat when everything was pushing them down, but also to transform themselves into better people than they were before the catastrophe.

Several of the people featured in this book were well-known before they experienced their crises: television journalist Mike Wallace; Jeb Stuart Magruder, central Watergate figure, now a senior Presbyterian minister; and prize-winning author Andre Dubus. Others became public figures and discovered new purposes in life because of the catastrophe that splintered their lives. The following list mentions only a few of their many accomplishments: Max Cleland, wounded Vietnam veteran and triple amputee, became Georgia's Secretary of State and authored a book about his ordeal; Holocaust survivor Elie Wiesel won the Nobel Peace Prize; former political prisoner Armando Valladares became a UN Ambassador; mastectomy survivor Deena Metzger became a psychotherapist, has written several books and became an inspiration to many breast-cancer victims because of the well-known poster on which she proudly displays her one-breasted chest; Anne Capute, tried but found innocent of killing a patient with a morphine overdose, became a media sensation (her ordeal was portrayed in the book *Fatal Dosage* and in a television movie); and Rabbi Harold Kushner wrote a hugely successful book (*When Bad Things Happen to Good People*) after the death of his son. A third group has led somewhat quieter lives (in terms of the media) but has provided a great amount of care and service to others: Eleanor and Dick Grace founded The Brain Center after their daughter died from a neurologic disease; MS survivor and paraplegic Alan Langer started a TV series (*Willing, Ready, Enable*); Donna

Jenkins is a child psychologist; after being injured in a car accident that left her paralyzed from the waist down, Nackey Loeb kept herself going after her husband died and now runs New Hampshire's state newspaper; Richard Herrmann is a university professor who inspires others to go after their dreams; clinical psychiatrist Patti Dean is a suicide and teen crisis counselor; and finally, Victor Davidoff, former political prisoner and the victim of ghastly mental torture, has found strength to go on when not only his body, but also his mind, was all but stolen from him.

It is interesting that each one of these very different characters — people from all walks of life with entirely different losses — used many of the same methods that were necessary to forge ahead when life seemed unbearable. This book explores the lives of these remarkable people. The interviews tap into their most personal terrain, the place where thoughts and roles are privately composed, where they make meaning of their world.

I think it is necessary to point out that the catastrophes suffered by those I interviewed are very extreme, far more so than anything most of us will hopefully ever have to experience, but this by no means implies that the resilience and inner strength these survivors were able to summon differ in substance from what is needed to face less catastrophic problems. Therefore, this book will be of benefit to anyone who suffers a catastrophe, whether life-threatening or not.

Although history is full of examples of people who found themselves in the midst of adversity, the psychological literature has focused primarily on the ravages of severe stress. The implication is that stress produces dysfunctional survivors, that emotional disability will inevitably follow trauma and that the survivors will feel they are "damaged goods." Positive transformation following trauma has been all but ignored. However, from the books I read and from the people with whom I spoke, I knew that many individuals have been able to convert adversity into triumph, and to emerge from shattering losses with more integrity, self-respect and a wider vision of the world than they had previously. Consider the following examples:

Harry Stack Sullivan, who became a distinguished psychiatrist, was suspended from Cornell University as an undergraduate and, soon after, suffered a schizophrenic episode. During his recovery, he studied mental illness and became determined to study medicine. His observations on schizophrenic states were illuminated by his own illness as were his many discoveries about effective treatment for the mentally ill. He is considered one of the most important figures in the history of American psychiatry.

Playwright Eugene O'Neill, depressed by a life of beachcombing, drunkenness and marital failure, attempted suicide as a young man. He believed that the act effectively "killed" his old self and he started over as a journalist. Soon, however, another crisis awaited him — a bout with tuberculosis. While recovering in a sanitarium, he decided that his life's mission was to write plays. O'Neill went on to become one of America's most outstanding playwrights.

Buckminster Fuller decided to devote his life to reforming the environment while standing on the shore of Lake Michigan, contemplating suicide. He looked out at the sharp, cold waves and suddenly recognized the exquisite design of life. He knew there was a greater intellect in the universe than his own and wondered if his life could contribute to the integrity of the universe. This vision sustained him through the difficult times ahead when he had to endure financial hardship to make his goal in architecture and design a reality.

Stephen Hawking, now a world-famous physicist, was struck with amyotrophic lateral sclerosis (Lou Gehrig's disease) while he was a university student. (This devastating, relentless neurologic disorder paralyzes skeletal muscles, affects speech and swallowing and usually ends in failure of the chest muscles to sustain respiration.) For two years Hawking did little work on his doctorate because he didn't believe that he would live very long. He stayed in his room listening to Wagner, reading science fiction and drinking. Then, in a paper he read on black holes in space written by Roger Penrose, Hawking found a problem that fascinated him. As he began working on it, the progression of his disease inexplicably slowed. Hawking now holds Sir Isaac Newton's chair as Lucasian Professor of Mathematics at Cambridge University. Although he is confined to a wheelchair and speaks by means of a computer that converts typed messages into a synthetic voice, he is regarded as the most brilliant theoretical physicist since Einstein. He says he is happier now than before the onset of his illness. "I was very bored with life. I drank a fair bit, I guess; I didn't do any work. When one's expectations are reduced to zero, one really appreciates everything one does have."

Writer Flannery O'Connor's life was redirected when she developed lupus, an incurable tissue disease. She learned the concept of "passive diminishment" — the serene acceptance of afflictions that cannot be changed by any means — from theologian Pierre Teilhard de Chardin. O'Connor wrote to Robert and Elizabeth Lowell, "I have enough energy to write with and as that is all I have any business doing anyhow, I can, with one eye squinted, take it all as a blessing."

Many people have worked through severe losses by using some form of creativity. Sigmund Freud wrote *The Interpretation of Dreams* as a way of mourning his father's death. Gustav Mahler used his musical genius to grieve for the death of his several siblings. Miguel de Cervantes' left arm was paralyzed from a wound he received in war. When he created the immortal Don Quixote, he said it was for the glory of his arm. Although James Joyce was nearly blind when he wrote *Ulysses*, he described the city of Dublin to the reader in a way he would like to have seen it himself. Painters Edgar Degas and Claude Monet both suffered from visual impairments, but that did not stop them from painting. Degas was unable to see long distances, so he concentrated on close-ups, in particular painting ballet dancers in extreme detail. Monet created his breath-taking "Water Lily" series while undergoing repeated eye operations for degenerative cataracts. Particularly inspiring is Beethoven, who after contracting syphilis, gradually became hard of hearing and eventually stone deaf. This must have been devastating to a man whose hearing was his life, but it did not hold him back. He could not hear a note as the orchestra played his Ninth Symphony, the last concert he conducted. So moving, so magnificent was Beethoven's premiere concert that night in Vienna that the entire audience rose to their feet and offered him a thundering ovation. Beethoven was facing the orchestra and therefore was not aware of what was happening. Moved to tears, the lead violinist walked over and literally turned Beethoven around to face the audience so that he could see — because he could not hear — the wild applause he was receiving. Incredibly, the best music Beethoven composed was probably during the second period of his life when he was completely deaf.

As noted, all of the people discussed in these pages made wrenching journeys to the edge of life, but all of them survived and were even transformed in the process. How did these heavily burdened individuals emotionally survive their trauma and how did they recast their lives? The stories in this book describe several trauma survivor's intimate thoughts about these questions. When I first listened to their stories, I was electrified as they stretched their psyches and unfolded their thoughts. As I retold their stories and described their journeys, I tried, whenever possible, to use their own words so that I could capture accurately the sentiments they felt. I hope my experience as a listener will mirror your experience as a reader.

We discover our most important inner potential by moving beyond our own selves and into something that is bigger than we are. When we go deep into another's "dark night of the soul," we touch something universal, something that connects us to each other and the rest of the world. The people I have written about and the stories they tell show that it is indeed possible to recover from trauma, that it does not necessarily lead to demise and finally, that it can even inspire emotional growth, allowing one to become a wiser, bigger person. These survivors show us that if we can endure the pain of endings — and every change in life brings with it an ending — then we can experience the also painful, yet immensely rewarding birth of a new life.

I am deeply grateful and honored for the privilege of interviewing these extraordinary individuals. I hope their words and thoughts will help others who face similar challenges to realize that rejuvenation — even in the face of life-threatening disintegration — is absolutely possible and that breakdown can become breakthrough.

Mary Baures

Andre Dubus

Andre Dubus' house is perched on a tree-covered hill in Haverhill, Massachusetts. On one side of the house, in a patch of soil polished by small feet, is a swing set. On the other side, a wheelchair ramp climbs to the upper level of the wooden house.

Inside the house, books and stuffed animals mingle on counter tops. Dubus, author of nine books of fiction, is sitting in his wheelchair in the kitchen. He has a Hemingwayesque beard, a weathered face and an exuberant voice within which a Southern accent still lingers. He is frying hamburgers while he talks to me about the physical and emotional struggles he's encountered since he was hit by a car a year earlier.

On July 23, 1986, Dubus was driving home from Boston on a four-lane segment of the highway. He was returning from a section of the city called the Combat Zone where he had been researching a story on a hooker. As he neared the town of Wilmington he spotted a car, headlights off, stopped in the middle of the third lane. A woman was standing beside the car. When Dubus noticed that she was crying and bleeding, he pulled over to the center guard rail to see whether he could offer assistance.

The woman, Luz Santiago, was Puerto Rican and neither she nor her brother, Luis, who suddenly appeared from the other side of the car, spoke much English. They had just hit a motorcycle that had been

1

left abandoned in the middle of the road. Dubus noticed
a pool of dark liquid at the Santiagos' feet and it seemed
to him that the driver of the motorcycle was trapped
beneath their car. (Dubus later learned that the liquid
was oil from the crankcase of the car, but then he
thought it was blood, that a serious accident had occurred and that these people needed serious help.) He
dreaded looking underneath the car and instead decided that he should first try to get some help. He
began to wave down oncoming drivers, one of whom
was a woman driving a Honda at nearly 60 mph. While
the exact reasons are unclear, instead of stopping to
help, she drove directly into Dubus and the Santiagos
who were all standing beside the car.

Dubus was able to push Luz Santiago out of the way
just in time, but her brother, hit head on by the speeding
Honda, was killed. Dubus, on the other hand, was alive,
but badly injured. After his internal injuries were no
longer life-threatening, he spent two months in Massachusetts General Hospital during which time he had 11
operations. One of his legs had to be amputated at the
knee and the bones of the other were shattered. The
woman who hit Dubus never contacted him, never even
sent him a card even though she was fully aware of the
severity of his injuries. She was not drunk at the time of
the accident and escaped prosecution. This lack of concern caused Dubus to hate her for a long time.

Now, 13 months after the accident, there is a red sock on
the leg that was shattered and an ace bandage on the
stump of the leg that was amputated. He's in gym shorts
and a T-shirt, ready for his late afternoon workout. The
muscles in his arms are evidence that he exercises a lot.

His mouth seems to taste amusement as he wheels
around the kitchen, pivoting from refrigerator to stove
and back again, stretching to retrieve things almost out
of his reach. There's something special about this afternoon. For the first time since the accident, he is taking
care of himself; Dubus' wife and children have gone to

visit her father, leaving him alone at home. Although friends offered to stay with him, he wanted to prove to himself that he could function alone once again. His spirit is thriving on this exercise of independence.

"If I hadn't had a family, I would have died," he says. "Just after I was hit and was close to death and fighting for my life, the desire to be with my family was there, while giving up might have been there. I had [thoughts of my wife] Peggy and [my daughter] Cadence inside of me instead of despair. I can remember when I was in intensive care and Peggy whispered into my ear for me to try to clear my lungs. I knew that things were serious because my lungs were filling up with fluid. I couldn't talk, but somehow my body felt better when she was there. My blood pressure also went down."

Dubus spent over five years in the Marines and he is able to use the skills that he learned, especially in combat. "Marines don't fight for their country. They fight because they love each other; they don't want to let their buddies down. Peggy's a writer [*When the Animals Leave* is one of her published books], and she was doing workshops when I was hit. She didn't write from June to April, and to go unfulfilled as a writer is hard.

After Dubus got home from the hospital he was dependent on his wife, who cared for him diligently. He had diarrhea for several weeks and Peggy, who was pregnant, had to clean him. By the time she had put their daughter and her husband to bed, she was too spent to read or write. To make matters worse, every night, just as the sun began to fade, Dubus had "the terrors." He was hit at night and is sure that there's some connection. But even when she wasn't cleaning her husband, life was difficult for Peggy. "One night, my wife said that we lost what we had in the hospital. We got remarried in the hospital when she brought my ring back. Dubus remembers telling her, "What you are going through now is greater. When I was in the hospital, I was helpless. I couldn't move. I had needles stuck in my arm. Everything you did then was a sacrament. The outside sign of the giving of grace. Now you are living with a man who has his strength back, but he can't walk. So you get a man who grieves and is pissed off and desperate and cranky. A man who has lust and passion. A man who yells and cries because he can't go outside and walk. What we are doing now is harder," he said, "because it's spiritual *and* physical. Now it is the way it should be."

"Peggy kept worrying that the baby in her womb was receiving signals that things weren't good. Having the baby was supposed to be the major joy in her life this year, but things were so hard here, she just went to the hospital and did it. Painfully. But the baby, Madeleine, came out peaceful. A few months ago Peggy said, 'There's something I haven't told you about Madeleine. There's a look she gives me that is pure love.' Peggy once told me of a story she read that was about children being close to God. Peggy thinks a part of Madeleine is still on the other side; in other words, very close to God. Peggy gets angry with God for what happened to me, but she can then look at Madeleine and be soothed. I told her that she always knew there was more to life than errands, shit and sex. There's a lot more going on.

"My wife seems to be on a spiritual quest. I'm lucky I'm Catholic, so I never lost faith. She was always in touch with God, but she didn't know it. I define 'belief' as belief in God and 'faith' as God believing in you. It's like the difference between being lonely in Boston and being alone in Boston when the person who loves you very much is in Los Angeles. There's a big difference.

"The story isn't that Madeleine brought to Peggy an emotional connection she needed. The story isn't that she was in touch with God—that would be too simple. [It was that] God wasn't in touch with her. There was never one single event that changed my attitude and direction like in the movies. There has been a whole 13 months of recovery and it is still going on.

"We had a very hard time in June when they took the cast off my good leg. It became clear that everything was terrible. Things looked so bad, and obviously, whatever we were waiting for wasn't going to happen. There wasn't going to be a summer this year. We used to spend the summer writing, working out, going to the beach and buying fish on the way home.

"I wrote a passage about what spring is like when you are too old or too depressed to partake of its beauty. What you do is look out the window and yearn for it because you can't have it.

"For seven weeks, all of June and most of July, I grieved. Then things started to happen. Spiritual things. My wife solved my temporary impotence and I began to feel some sensation in my leg. You've heard of phantom limb. The feeling in my leg came back to me during a post-orgasmic release; suddenly I could feel every toe and muscle. Right then I got my spirit back."

Dubus says that physical love between a man and a woman is a sacrament in which their nakedness is not only physical, but also emotional, spiritual and mental. It's "where your sin is my sin, your evil my evil, your weakness my weakness. The beloved always knows that he or she is loved by the lover despite anything that happens. It is a high state, a very high state."

With the healing power that this communion with his wife had on his spirit, Dubus felt ready to begin working on his body. "I wheeled myself into my physical therapist's office and she started working on my leg. It looks more like a leg now, but it was a piece of shit when she first started to treat it." He grasps his leg where the calf muscle is developing. Now the red sock looks festive to me, a way of celebrating his new muscles. "When I first got home from the hospital, I looked the way my father looked the day before he died of cancer. I weighed 130 pounds and I couldn't even lift my tiny daughter Cadence who weighed only 42 pounds at the time."

As Dubus illustrates some of his exercises, his neck becomes a coil of tendons and his shoulders bunch up. When he reaches up to grab an imaginary bar, his stump shoots out. "At first I had a hard time keeping my balance, but then the stump began to lift. The stump knows what to do.

"You learn patience when you are a cripple, but the real strength belongs to Peggy. She's had to lead the life of two adults. Just running errands can take up a whole day. It's not that she gained something she didn't have before, but what was latent in her before was forced to become active and, as a result, she grew. That's true with most human beings. You have potential and something happens to make you use it.

"Last week my wife was crying and of course I thought I'd done something wrong, but she said no, 'Everyday is just so hard.' Everything takes so long and it's hard. On the other hand," Dubus said, "there have been so many spiritual gifts that have come to us—especially people's love."

John Irving, who only knew Dubus through his work, was so moved by Dubus' accident that he called some of his friends—Kurt Vonnegut, John Updike, Stephen King, Tim O'Brien, E.L. Doctorow, Richard Yates and others to start an organization called The Friends of Andre Dubus Literary Series. They held a series of readings at the Charles Hotel in Cambridge and all of those who attended paid $50 each. This money was given to Dubus to help defray his staggering medical expenses. Although Dubus knew Vonnegut and Yates from the Writer's Workshop at the University of Iowa and Doctorow from Dial Press, he did not know the others who donated their time and money. Their support, he feels, was an enormous spiritual gift.

But for Dubus, the biggest spiritual gift was witnessing his wife and children come through suffering. "Cadence, who is five this year, is my little playmate. She comes home from school to play with me, and I always say, 'Have I told you today that I love you?' She always says 'Yes, but you can say it again.'" His mouth becomes a circle of delight as he speaks of Cadence, but this warm bubble of emotion suddenly breaks and he becomes pensive again. He sets the spatula down, turns from the stove, and stares. "I told Cadence, 'Most girls don't have their daddy go out and end up in the hospital or their pregnant mommy leave home from 1 to 10 p.m. every da to go to the hospital [to visit her injured husband]. And most girls don't have their daddies come home in a cast and sleep in a hospital bed and use a bed pan and have somebody else cut the Christmas tree. I tell her, 'When you grow up somebody is gonna have to work awfully hard to make you unhappy 'cause you're a strong girl, a strong girl.'" A tear rolls down the side of his nose, but he quickly wipes it away.

The hamburgers are now finished. Dubus lifts one onto a paper plate, scoops on some beans and places the plate, ketchup, napkins and silverware in his lap. He pivots away from the stove, and wheels into the dining room where his dog Luke is waiting. As Dubus lifts the plate to the table, it bends, spilling some of the beans onto the floor. "Next time I'll know not to use a paper plate," he says. But it is lucky for Luke who makes moist noises of appreciation at the beans before licking them up.

A large window looks onto a view of the sky and leafy branches. The dining room overlooks the living room and both are filled with humble furniture and utilitarian objects: books, paper, vitamins and toys. Dubus' house is a place where people really live; it is not a showplace. He is very aware of the difference between people who place a high value on material things and those who value people instead. Dubus is clearly a member of the latter group. In fact, one of the themes of his work is that our culture has been corrupted because of peoples' overwhelming lust for material things. He feels many develop a sense of worthlessness when they see that others have things that they do not.

During his development as a writer, Dubus deliberately did without any unnecessary comforts. In 1964, when he went to Iowa where he began work on his master's degree in writing, he lived on $2400 a year and Dubus even sold his blood for $25 a pint.

After the publication of his first novel, *The Lieuten-*

ant, a story about the moral crisis of a contingent of
Marines, Dubus and his family moved back to the north-
east part of the country where he began to teach. "I would
rather be broke in Massachusetts than wealthy in Ne-
braska," he says.

Dubus' work is about the many faces of love, including the dark side. His characters are frequently trapped
between despair and responsibility and they often live in
tortured circumstances. They are capable of beauty and
nobility, but often find it easier to settle for jobs they don't
like and marriages that are loveless. Since honorable
behavior is of ultimate importance to Dubus, he is particularly pleased by the strength that has emerged in his
wife Peggy since the accident. Many people, he is well
aware, leave when the going gets tough.

After Dubus came home from the hospital, his wife
said to him that she felt they had lost something very
important in their marriage because of Dubus' accident
and the long ordeal at the hospital. "I wanted to soothe
her, and I said, 'What you are going through now [that I
am home] is greater. When I was in the hospital, I was
helpless. I couldn't move. I had needles stuck in my arm.
I told her, 'Everything you did then was a sacrament. The
outward sign of the giving of grace.'

"Making a sandwich can be a sacrament if you do it
right. As D.H. Lawrence said, a woman in love does not
mind her housework—although he said it better. I tried
to write about that in *Adultery*. When a woman is cleaning
the place of a dying man, it's not cleaning the place [so
much as it is giving] a gift. In the same way, my wife's
getting in the car everyday to visit me was a spiritual gift."

Dubus tried to defuse his depression by not taking
what he felt when he was down too seriously. "Everything
is out of proportion [when one is depressed]. It's like being
drunk. Considering all the things that could have happened I feel very fortunate. Suppose the lady had hit me
with a truck instead of a Honda, I could have been killed,
or I could have been paralyzed or my genitals could have
been damaged."

"Also, you have to consider the nature of my work. I'm not a ball player, I'm a writer. There was this kid in New York, a hockey player, who committed suicide after losing a leg. [Had he lived] he could have coached and maybe even played hockey again. And then there's this guy in New Zealand who runs, or rather hops, the marathon. With examples like that it's hard to feel sorry for a guy who commits suicide after losing a leg. The point I'm making is that people can make do."

Another way that Dubus puts the accident and the ensuing loss of his mobility into perspective is by comparing it to other losses. For example, he doesn't feel that the accident is as bad as when his first family, which he started when he was in his twenties first broke up. Not being able to live with his four children "hurt worse than losing the damn leg."

Dubus' attempts to understand what happened to him echo the dialogue of one of his characters in *Voices from the Moon*. A mother, speaking to her distraught son, says, "You know why I like my waitress friends so much? And what I learned from them? They don't have delusions. So when I'm alone at night—and I love it, Larry, I look out my window, and it comes to me; we don't have to live great lives, we just have to understand and survive the ones we've got."

Some of the major things Dubus now understands about life are that people need to have a harmonious center within and that they need to believe in something more than and greater than themselves. At the beginning of *Adultery and Other Choices* Dubus quotes Anton Chekhov: "Unless a man has something stronger, something superior to all outside influences, he only needs to catch a bad cold to lose his balance entirely, to take every bird for a fowl of ill omen, and to hear the baying of hounds in every noise, while his pessimism or his optimism, together with all his thoughts, great or small, are significant solely as symptoms and in no other way."

"Chekhov did not believe in God," Dubus explains. His lunch finished, he lights up a Lucky Strike which he keeps in a canvas bag. Waving the hand holding the cigarette in the air, he wheels himself in slow circles with the other. "But he believed that everyone needs a god greater than himself. He wrote a story about a brilliant doctor and lecturer, who, because of his failure to love, never had anything greater than himself. All his opinions were just symptoms of his emptiness."

Dubus seems to feel that if one's god is oneself, then one's god is an idol without a soul. Dubus says he stays in touch with his soul by having a family and work that he loves and a strong faith in god. "My family is my first vocation. I've been a father since four days after my twenty-second birthday. It's great to be a father. I'm always worried about one of my children and it keeps me connected to the universe."

Dubus' belief in people's need for something greater than themselves makes him discouraged in the changes that he has seen in the American culture during his lifetime. "People are concerned about three things: fear of dying, greed and vanity. They are very unconnected with nature. My son Andre gave me a copy of a 1963 *Saturday Evening Post* and the first thing I looked at were the advertisements. There were no diet products and some women in bathing suits on the beach did not have bones poking through their skin. There were no anorexic models. When I was growing up women like Jane Russell and Marilyn Monroe were normal. My mother was normal. And when people talked about fat, they meant *FAT*.

"Now we have clothes designed by New York homosexuals who want women to look like boys. But the real evil is that women try to shape themselves to fit these images. People don't have any strength when they are too thin—it's not natural for women to be bony. I know bulimics. These people are not happy. I have a friend whose daughter is anorexic, and it is no joke. These people have no center. They worry all the time about what other people think of them." He believes that our culture encourages a neurotic relationship with our bodies.

"If you worry so much about what other people think

of you, you only live in their imagination. When they are not thinking of you, you don't exist. When you have no integrity and no center, you are a whore. We used to use this word a lot. It means becoming what other people want you to be because of their money, or power you think you have to have. You give up your whole identity.

"Compared to that, losing my goddamn leg isn't terrible. I would rather be crippled than sick in my soul. I would rather have my problems than to not be right with my soul."

The second conversation I had with Dubus was a year later and by that time he had suffered still another serious loss. In November 1987, his wife Peggy left him. Because the judge did not feel that he could care for small children, she took Cadence and Madeleine with her.

The children visit him only twice a month, but their presence is everywhere at his house: a rubber pool is on the porch, filled up with air and in it are a rubber pony and an inflatable bear and a waist-high tepee is set up on the dining room floor next to his barbells. Painted on the living room bookcase is a poem to Cadence, "A worm climbs out of the sea onto the wings of love."

A red sweatband brightens Dubus' head; he has just finished his afternoon workout. In his wheelchair, decorated with a Marine decal, he looks out at the panorama of trees and the clear blue sky. He seems pensive as he remembers other summers of swimming, fishing and going to Fenway Park. And, of course, he remembers that he had the companionship of his wife and daughters.

Ever since experiencing the pain of his wife leaving, and with her, their two children, Dubus has been unable to write. "I can deal with the gimp stuff, but my heart's broken by not having my kids here. When you are a cripple it's important not to be self absorbed, to get out of yourself."

Dubus' losses reverberate against each other; his lost mobility makes his lost marriage and the ensuing lost connection with his children worse, and finally the lost ability to give birth to stories.

He hangs onto his dignity even when his will power proves inadequate. To prevent his sadness and grief from getting out of proportion, Dubus goes to Mass every morning where he is able to get a better perspective on his depression. "I get a sense of my place in time [by performing and experiencing] rituals that have been going on for 2000 years. The image of that man stretched out on the cross lets me know that life wasn't supposed to be easy. Of course, I always knew it would be hard, but I never expected it to be this hard."

Of his wife's departure, he says, "She got tried, and I won't say that she failed, but her direction changed." One of his stories begins with a quote that love is not a state of the soul, but a direction. It is a place where one can arrive at, but also a place that one can leave. Dubus remembers the turning point when something seemed to disappear from their marriage. He had been foul with diarrhea for three weeks. Each cleaning Peggy gave him took 30 minutes and she always went to bed exhausted.

The marriage, his second, was over after Peggy left him, saying she wanted a divorce. When Dubus' lawyer called him to say that his wife would soon be coming with a court order and a police officer to get the girls, Dubus and Cadence were playing with stuffed bears. Dubus played a giant with a deep voice who had lost a leg and Cadence, who provided the voices for the animals, became creatures with missing or wounded limbs who needed healing and the giant's love. The stuffed-bear games became a sacrament that sustained life and had an tender ambiance of magic.

Dubus had to explain to Cadence that her mother was coming with a policeman to take her and that her mother, like a good momma bear, was doing what she felt was right. Cadence tightened her little fist around a piece of apron from her Raggedy Anne doll, swung one of the bears into Dubus' lap and, with her thumb in her mouth, went into her room and shut the door.

Dubus wheeled himself through her door at an angle and saw her above him up on the top part of her bunk bed, sucking her thumb with tears in her eyes. Dubus had told his physical therapist he wanted to learn to climb the ladder to her bed but was told that he wasn't ready yet. Dubus said to himself, "To hell with this crippled shit." Holding the wooden side of the bunk, he lifted his body up and pivoted onto the mattress beside his daughter. Cadence sat up and was grinning. "Daddy, you got up here!" Cadence's sadness was momentarily pushed aside by surprise and glee over her father's expanded mobility.

Dubus seems sadder now then when we conversed a year ago. Fortunately that sadness had not made him withdraw; he still reaches out to others. After Peggy left, he had constant phone conversations with his friend Jack Herlihy, the manager of a local bookstore. Herlihy is now living in Dubus' house. He says he is amazed at Dubus' refusal to be morose in the face of all that has happened to him and he admires his humor, which enables him to place his losses in perspective without making them seem trivial.

A writer friend then drops by and Dubus seems to liven up. Dubus is once again in a favorite element—telling stories in front of an attentive audience. With salty speech, laughing gleefully, he tells a story about a quadriplegic friend who tries to take on a gang of punks in a bar.

Many of his stories now dramatize that courage is not synonymous with physical strength. In his boyhood, Dubus thought his small size attracted bullies. After he had transformed his body with construction work, however, he realized that it was his fear of public humiliation that attracted bullies to him. He learned to confront bullies because something in him demanded respect and even if the confrontation caused him injuries, that was not nearly as bad as cowardice. Now, as he is still adjusting to his broken body, he needs to remind himself of that lesson.

On Bastille Day, not long after my second chat with Dubus, he had received a MacArthur Fellowship, which honors highly creative individuals whose work is considered important to support. The fellowship included a $310,000 stipend. This set him free financially. At once he used the money to hire a housekeeper and to build a lap pool in his yard so that he wouldn't have to contend with the beach, where the wheels of his wheelchair stuck in the sand. He also bought a new Toyota Celica with a cellular phone. He also had a special rig built on the roof of the car that lifts, lowers and unfolds, and deposits his wheelchair on the ground by the door of his vehicle. Winning the MacArthur seemed to boost Dubus' morale and reminded him of his commitment to writing. After medical technology had replaced some of his lost mobility and domestic help freed up his time, Dubus was able to write again.

In a collection of essays, *Broken Vessels,* published in July 1991, Dubus describes his physical and spiritual transformations since his accident. In the title essay he begins in a suicidal black hole where he fights against the darkness. Every day he read a passage from the New Testament. He writes, "Whoever receives this little child for my sake, receives me," and describes how he inspired deep communion with his children, and through it he learned to give and receive strength and love. Thus, he finds a connection to the miraculous and climbs triumphantly out the abyss. At one point in the essay, Dubus, who lived much of his adult life protecting those more vulnerable than himself, writes that he had to watch helplessly while his daughter Madeleine crawled down a ramp toward an exercise bicycle, oblivious to shouted warnings, and stuck her finger in the moving chain, severing the tip of the finger.

After Madeleine was rushed to the hospital, Dubus told Cadence how brave she was when her sister got hurt. Cadence asked him why so many hurtful things happen to their family and momentarily Dubus is lost for words. Finally, he says "I don't know, but you're getting awfully good at [coping with] it."

Just as Dubus learned to receive strength from his children, he was also forced to rethink his concept of manhood. The instinct to risk himself for others was molded into his character when he was in the Marines, but the mold cracked that night when he stopped along the highway to help two stranded motorists.... It is clear that Dubus, no longer a physically powerful Marine, has to contend with his inability to defend himself and those he cares about. In his book, *Broken Vessels*, Dubus describes a group of teenagers who disturb him and his wife at a movie. His wife asks them to please stop talking. Dubus is silent and feels helpless. After one of the teenagers harrasses his wife, Dubus tells him to cool off. As the movie ends, Dubus thinks to himself, "If he insulted me, I would pull him down to me and punch him." But the teenager walks past him, looking down and avoiding eye contact. Filled with shame, the adrenaline went out of Dubus. "If you confront a man from a wheelchair, you're bullying him. Only a coward would hit a man in a chair."

Also described in *Broken Vessels* is a conversation Dubus has with a woman who, upon seeing him in a wheelchair, shows compassion by "laying down the shield and sword she had learned to carry" on the aggressive New York City streets. Dubus says that there is a universality to a wounded person that draws tenderness from others and also enables him to see more clearly the suffering and crippling of those whose bodies are whole.

At the end of the book Dubus claims that he has finally learned to embrace whatever remains after the losses that have torn their way though his life have calmed. Like his daughters, Dubus suffered—and still suffers—terribly from those losses, but he endures and has found joy and harmony in his life. All of us, Dubus says, suffer cripplings. The key is to realize that we need each other to pick ourselves up and progress to a higher state of wisdom and humanity.

Elie Wiesel

Whenever Holocaust survivor Elie Wiesel discovers a place where his opinions on the subject of human dignity need to be heard, he speaks his mind. It is, Wiesel says, perhaps only "a small voice, maybe only heard by a few," but he is modest. His message is important and it needs to be told. And the world listens; in 1986, Wiesel won the Nobel Peace Prize and was praised as one of the "most important spiritual leaders and guides in an age when violence, repression and racism continue to characterize the world."

Wiesel devotes much of his energy to helping those in need. In 1986, he negotiated with Soviet leader Mikhail Gorbachev to give a group of Soviet Jews the freedom to emigrate from Russia. He was instrumental in helping dissident physicist Andrei Sakharov return to Moscow. He has used his position to help various other groups: Cambodian refugees, the Miskito Indians of Nicaragua and the starving children in Africa. Wiesel wonders why, when the prisoners in the Nazi death camps so desperately needed the help of others, the rest of the world was so silent.

Nazi ideology was built on the concept that by forcing certain attitudes and behaviors on people, it would reduce them to apathy; and indeed, one of the Nazis' objectives was to try to extinguish all humanity from their prisoners. In an essay Wiesel wrote, he says: "A few beatings, a few screams turned [a person] into a blank...his loss of identity [would become] complete.... Camp law and camp truth transcended all laws and all truths, and the prisoner could not help but submit." But, while imprisoned, Wiesel gradually realized that those who had the strength to care for others had a better chance of surviving emotionally, spiritually, morally and physically. He has carried this thought with him ever since. Wiesel's message is modest, humble and gets right at the heart of the matter: "People can help themselves by helping others. The opposite of love is not hate, but indifference. The opposite of art is not ugliness, but indifference. The opposite of life is not death, but indifference to life and to death."

Elie Wiesel's office at Boston University is six floors above the School of Theology. There he meets with students, prepares his lectures and writes. His office looks like his writing sounds: austere, stark and serious.

Surrounded by bare white walls adorned only by a clock and shelves crammed with books, Wiesel spends his time exploring the dark and ambiguous caves of the human psyche. From here, he shouts to a relatively deaf world about the plight of six million Jews who died in the Nazi death camps. He tries to rouse the world from self-concern and indifference to man's inhumanity to man. To write about evil, he believes, is to fight it. He also feels strongly that today's children need to know about the atrocities that have occurred in the past so that history will not repeat itself.

Unlike the subjects of some of the books he has written, Wiesel does not seem to pulsate with sadness when he speaks to me. But the sadness is there. Big, black holes of it that leave a trace in his smile.

We are discussing healing. Wiesel tells me that he does not consider himself "healed" from the wounds inflicted by the Nazis on him and all the other Jewish victims of the Holocaust.

I explain that by healing I don't mean that the loss

doesn't still hurt or that it disappears, but that there is a way that people can find some meaning in a catastrophe so they can go on with their lives.

"Being healed," he says, "is when the wound is no longer there." We both laugh. His ability to communicate simply and eloquently is a pleasure. "In a strange way I never wanted to be healed," he explains. For Wiesel, being "healed" is too much like forgetting.

His manner is gentle and gracious and in a soft way he tells me that he belongs to a generation that does not believe in the healing process that we have just been talking about. To follow his thought process, the listener must combine one thought with its opposite. But his contradictions blend together smoothly and the fissures end up being invisible and once joined together, his thoughts often wind up as questions.

"Questions are important," he says. "I don't have answers, but I have questions. They give us dignity and power and hope to go on living. Questions are very important to ourselves and to God." The questions he asks reverberate deep within the listener, and since much of his thinking is dialectical, he offers no neat solutions or clear answers. This is something Wiesel is very aware of; in fact, he is steadfast in his opinion that there are no neat solutions or answers to very many things in this world. And regarding the Holocaust, the very suggestion of simple explanations is abhorrent.

"Auschwitz was not a God-made kingdom sent down from Heaven. Auschwitz was created by man, for man and against man. How could human beings *imagine* something like that? And then *do* it?" The Nazis turned murder into a science, a procedure that incorporated specialized laboratories, progress charts and business meetings. Many of the Nazi murderers had university degrees in philosophy, biology, medicine, the fine arts and even theology. That the taste for bloodshed seems so antithetical to most of these individuals' social and cultural backgrounds and spiritual legacies, that it was possible to fire a gun at living humans and still be capable of appreciating the aesthetic aspects of life—the cadence of a poem or the composition of a painting, is especially incomprehensible to Wiesel. Adolf Eichmann, for instance, was an exemplary father and a considerate husband. But during the trial in Jerusalem, Eichmann spoke with cool detachment as he disclosed murder dates and associated information. Eichmann was devoid of vehemence or irony. He claimed that he was not an anti-Semite and Wiesel believes that he was being honest. To Eichmann, Jews had become simply objects and numbers that were to be annihilated. While Wiesel listened to Eichmann's testimony, he decided that if Eichmann were sane, he himself would easily choose to be mad.

Madness has a mystical appeal to Wiesel. "Madness is a question, not an answer," he says. "What separates life from death? Madness from truth?" He also believes that "the path to enlightenment [runs] through the ravaged landscape of madness."

Wiesel's writings are full of madmen who learn to grasp larger truths. They are reminiscent of Moshe, a witness who escaped a Jewish massacre when Wiesel was a boy in Sighet. Moshe tried to sound an alarm after the Gestapo stopped a train of Jewish deportees and forced them to dig huge graves. Then, they slaughtered all the deportees. Babies were thrown into the air and were used as machine gun targets. Moshe, who had only been wounded in the leg, was mistakenly left for dead, but he survived. He believed that he'd been miraculously kept alive so that he could warn others of the dangers of the approaching Nazis. But, when Moshe tried to tell his story, the townspeople thought he was mad and paid no attention to his warnings. Incidents such as the slaughter Moshe described seemed inconceivable to the Jews of Sighet and they had faith that such horrific things were impossible in a civilized world. How mistaken they were.

The madmen in Wiesel's books are "pure and beautiful." They have keen powers of perception and reject easy paths for hard ones. They make decisions in favor of God and man. Because they are able to break free of well-traveled thoughts, they don't fit in with the rest of society and are frequently captured by evil forces.

Wiesel was born in 1928 in Sighet, a small Romanian shtetl in the Carpathian Mountains. He was reborn, he says, in 1944 in a Nazi death camp strewn with corpses. On his second birth, he was given a new name, A-7713, a symbol that is still tattooed on his arm.

In 1944, when Wiesel was 15, he and his family were rounded up by the Nazis and sent to a ghetto. Wiesel's father had a friend who was a police officer. The friend promised to inform Wiesel's father if anything serious was about to happen. One night, someone knocked several times on the wooden boards that the Nazis had nailed across their windows, but Wiesel's father was not home, and his family was afraid to answer. Wiesel believes that it was his father's friend who had come to warn them of what was soon to come.

After a few weeks in the ghetto, the deportation started, with Adolf Eichmann personally supervising. The military police brutally struck men, women and children as they herded them like cattle into the sealed trains. Wiesel will always remember the indifferent look on the faces of his non-Jewish neighbors, who were left alone: "No shock and no sadness, no pain."

In spite of the their pain and fear, their tears and their bloody faces, they all remained silent during the entire procedure. Wiesel hoped that somehow this silence would bring triumph; silence, he believes, is mightier than language, beyond lies and beyond time. Hopefully, he felt, their silent prayers would stop the Gestapo brutality. However, nothing the Jews did made any difference. Their fates were already determined.

The Jews were loaded into cattle cars, uninformed of where they were going or what was going to happen to them. Wiesel's grandmother was the only one who seemed to know she was on her last journey; prepared, underneath her clothes she wore her *tachrichim*, her funeral clothes.

When they arrived at Auschwitz, a woman let out a cry when she heard dogs barking outside the train. Not a moment passed before she was silenced to death by a bullet. In the distance, smoke stacks spewed out red and yellow fire and dark smoke blackened the sky. Wiesel saw all the people and he saw the massive flames but did not know that the two would meet. When a man told Wiesel that they would all die in the fire, Wiesel remembers telling his father that something like that couldn't possibly occur in the twentieth century. As he later wrote, "Never shall I forget that night, the first night in camp, which has turned my life into one long night, seven times cursed and seven times sealed. Never shall I forget that smoke. Never shall I forget the little faces of children, whose bodies I saw turned into wreaths of smoke beneath a silent blue sky. Never shall I forget those flames which consumed my faith forever. Never shall I forget that nocturnal silence which deprived me, for all eternity, of the desire to live. Never shall I forget these moments which murdered my God and my soul and turned my dreams to dust. Never shall I forget these things, even if I am condemned to live as long as God Himself. Never."

Day after day, Wiesel was forced to watch his father's agony, his martyrdom and his slow death. Near the end, with puffy half-closed eyelids and animal terror in his eyes, Wiesel's father tried to speak. His cracked lips moved almost imperceptibly. Such a hideous death, Wiesel felt, was unreal and had no link to his father's life as he knew it and to the person his father had been.

Wiesel was not psychically armed for the evil he was now immersed in. As he watched the hanging of a child, death assumed the face of God. As François Mauriac writes about the ordeal in the foreword of Wiesel's book about the Holocaust, *Night*, "Have we ever thought about the consequences of a horror that, though less apparent, less striking than the other outrages, is yet the worst of all to those of us who have faith: the death of God in the soul of a child who suddenly discovers absolute evil?"

One of Wiesel's fellow campmates organized a tribunal of scholars who together decided to "put God on trial" in order to find out how God could allow such atrocities to occur. "How could one not ask certain questions?" Wiesel says. The outcome of the trial was that God was wrong, but afterward the group prayed to God anyway, or, as Wiesel puts it, "Maybe *for* God."

The trial's conclusion made a profound impression on Wiesel, who had grown up loving God, praying to God and making sure he was worthy of being His creature. He was deeply affected by the decision that had been reached about God in the trial, so he pushed the outcome—that God was wrong—into his subconscious. By then, he realized that God did not create Auschwitz, man did.

"I was not so much troubled by the behavior of man. What else could I expect of mankind with its history of cruelty, especially as seen by a Jewish boy? But God. God in all that, was a problem—*the* problem."

Sometimes Wiesel was convinced that if he survived, he would tell his story to the world and it would cause man to undergo a total metamorphosis—that something of the Messiah would appear in everyone.

By the time the Americans came, Wiesel was very close to death. Then, suddenly, he was free. "It was the most real and the most unreal day of my whole life." He hadn't eaten for days and a soldier offered him some Spam from his K-rations. When Wiesel brought the food to his lips, he fell unconscious. His body, he feels, protected him from eating pork, violating the Jewish teachings of his childhood.

With 400 other orphans, ages 6 to 18, Wiesel boarded a train bound for Belgium, but the train was diverted to France by General Charles de Gaulle who offered them shelter. At the border, passengers were asked whether they wished to become French citizens, but Wiesel was unable to understand French and as a result became stateless.

A Jewish organization provided a castle in Normandy in which the orphans could recuperate. They were divided into two groups: the religious and the non-religious.

Wiesel was in the religious group, which was sent to Ambloy. "We were beggars, unwanted everywhere," he explained in an essay, "condemned to exile and reminding strangers everywhere of what they had done to us and to themselves." Wiesel was filled with fear. "Fear of loving and of being rejected or loved for the wrong reasons, or for no reason at all. Marked, possessed…neither fully alive nor fully dead."

He began learning French and the new language became a symbol of a new beginning. Then, he threw himself into study and became fervently religious. "It was the best way to avoid the madness of the world outside life, outside Jewish life," he explains. "In reality, [there was nothing but] the cruel, sadistic madness, so the best way was to find the other madness, the healing one." He spent two years in an orphanage and then studied philosophy, literature and psychology at the Sorbonne, earning a living as a choir director, tutor, and translator. Later he went to India to write a dissertation on comparative asceticism which he never completed.

Wiesel knew that the task of a survivor was to testify, but he mistrusted the tools he had to use. Wiesel sees the Holocaust on a mystical plane, beyond human understanding. Through stories and tales, he struggles to articulate the ineffable. And although he uses words, he distrusts them, fearing that they might misrepresent or undermine the horror of what had really happened in the death camps, as well as undermining the intensity and urgency felt by those who were there. "How does one describe the indescribable? How does one use restraint in recreating the fall of mankind and the eclipse of the gods? And then, how can one be sure that the words, once uttered, will not betray, distort the message they bear?"

"So heavy was my anguish that I made a vow not to speak, not to touch upon the essential for at least ten years. Long enough to see clearly. Long enough to learn to listen to the voices crying inside my own. Long enough to learn to regain possession of my memory. Long enough to unite the language of man with the silence of the dead.

Maybe in a mystical way I thought I could purify language before using it for the sacred purpose of communicating the uncommunicable."

Wiesel was then hired as a French correspondent for an Israeli newspaper. The press cards that came with the job enabled him to accept assignments in Europe, America, North Africa and in the Orient. Homeless, he moved from one country to another and from one experience to another. He reported on the first Israeli-German claims conference "in such a way that nobody could have guessed that the negotiations for economic reparations concerned me much more than they did either group of delegates."

In 1954, in an interview with François Mauriac, Wiesel broke his oath of silence. After Mauriac gave an impassioned monologue on the theme of Christ, Wiesel uncharacteristically gave way to an angry impulse, closed his notebook and rose. "Sir," he said, "you speak of Christ. Christians love to speak of him. The passion of Christ, the agony of Christ, the death of Christ. In your religion, that is all you speak of. Well, I want you to know that ten years ago, not very far from here, I knew Jewish children, every one of whom suffered a thousand times more, six million times more than Christ on the cross. And we don't speak about them...."

Mauriac turned pale and slumped on the sofa, waiting for what Wiesel would say next, but Wiesel felt ill at ease and did not feel like continuing and left abruptly. While Wiesel was waiting for the elevator, he heard the door opening behind him, and Mauriac humbly touched his arm and asked him to come back.

When they returned to the drawing room, Mauriac began to cry. As tears streamed down his face, the old writer did nothing to stop them. He never took his eyes off Wiesel, who was mortified and overcome with remorse for having disturbed this fine man of heart and conscience.

Softly, Mauriac questioned Wiesel, and with considerable effort Wiesel answered in brief, staccato sentences:

"Yes, I come from that country. Yes, I lived through those events. Yes, I have known the sealed trains. Yes, I have seen darkness cover man's faith. Yes, I was present at the end of the world."

As Mauriac escorted him to the door and embraced him, he said, "I think that you are wrong. You are wrong not to speak.... Listen to the old man that I am: one must speak out—one must *also* speak out."

Wiesel feels that he grew close to Mauriac because the man recognized that there *was* Christian responsibility for the concentration camps. A year after the interview, Wiesel sent Mauriac his manuscript of *Night* and Mauriac personally found a publisher for the book. In the foreword, Mauriac gives his view of their first encounter. He describes Wiesel as looking like "a Lazarus risen from the dead, yet still a prisoner within the grim confines where he had stayed, stumbling among the shameful corpses."

After his initial silence, the floodgates open and Wiesel writes tirelessly and emphatically about human suffering. "In remembering cruelty, you fight cruelty; in telling the story of despair, you fight despair; in evoking the story of death, you serve the cause of humanity, which is to go on working, creating and living."

"Some people have written—wrongly—that I write to obtain a catharsis, but that is nonsense." It *is* nonsense because Wiesel does not want his wounds to be healed. Wiesel writes to create a dialogue, an "I and thou" relationship between his characters and between Wiesel and the reader. Wiesel says, too, that he writes in order not to go mad, or, on the contrary, to touch the bottom of madness. He says he entered literature through silence. By probing silence he discovered the perils and power of the word, and writing gave meaning to his survival and has justified each moment of his life. Wiesel says his main theme is not the Holocaust. "It would be harmful to turn that theme into a routine. Auschwitz and art are incompatible. I write about other subjects in order not to write about it; however, it *is* present. How could it not be present?"

By writing, the profound energy of Wiesel's experiences in the Nazi death camps has been transformed into a proliferation of imaginative artistic forms that have enabled Wiesel to explore abysses that defy understanding. He accepts the Holocaust as a sacred mystery. Wiesel warns, "One enters that territory like Moses in the presence of God—barefoot and trembling in one's being." Quoting Kafka, Wiesel says, "writing is a form of prayer." To Wiesel, prayer is a selection of certain words against others, a zone of piety and expectation surrounded by waiting and silence.

By writing about human suffering, Wiesel has found a task worthy of his powers and of his vision. He found an endeavor that enabled him to express himself passionately and to descend into underground springs where the waters are constantly renewed. Through writing, he is able to find harmonies and symbolic order.

In 1962, the same year that his book *The Accident* was published, Wiesel returned to Germany. He made this pilgrimage to relive the moment that had changed his life, and to confront the self he left behind in the death camps and the other self that he thought had survived.

After Wiesel checked into a run-down hotel, he went into the street and ran to his old house "as a convict runs toward freedom, as a madman runs toward his madness." As he wandered around outside, he felt vulnerable and invincible at the same time. The street, the yard, the gate were all the same. Only the Jews had disappeared.

The iron handle of the gate gave a familiar squeak. As he went into the yard, the sharp bark of a dog stopped him, bringing back old horrors. Wiesel had always considered dogs as friends of the enemy, so he took flight, running to the main street where he collapsed on a bench.

In the morning, he walked around the town and mingled with the people, but they were indifferent to him. The only place he felt at home was in the cemetery where he felt nestled in the bosom of a powerful family.

One of the people Wiesel showed his despair to was Ronald Reagan. In 1985 at the White House, Elie Wiesel, who says he is a shy, timid person, spoke to the President of the United States about morality on national television.

Wiesel had just been awarded a Congressional Gold Medal for his books about the savagery of the Nazis and the courage of their victims. The thin, gentle, wispy-haired survivor of the death camps graciously accepted the medal and then handed it to his 12-year-old son, Elisha. Turning to President Reagan, while senators and congressmen looked on, Wiesel implored him not to visit the SS graves in Bitberg, Germany.

"That place, Mr. President, is not your place. Your place is with the victims of the SS." Reagan listened with tight-lipped attention and pinched eyes. Much of what Wiesel says is difficult for others to hear. With passion and simple eloquence Wiesel continued, "The issue here is not politics, but good and evil. And we must never confuse them, for I have seen the SS at work and I have seen their victims…. Sons watched helplessly as their fathers were beaten to death. Mothers watched their children die of hunger. There was terror, fear, isolation, torture, gas chambers, flames rising to the heavens."

Reagan went to the graves anyway, but his visit created a furor. And while Reagan ignored Wiesel's plea, which pointed to the disrespect such a visit would show to those who perished at the hands of the SS, it nevertheless had lasting resonance.

Whatever inspired Reagan to ignore Wiesel's plea may have been operating when both Churchill and Roosevelt ignored the fate of the Jews during World War II. Wiesel is angry with both Roosevelt and Churchill, who, he says, were great human beings but "when it came to saving Jews, something happened to them."

More recently, Wiesel has sponsored a series of conferences on "The Anatomy of Hate," but realizes that to reduce the camps to something like hate is far too simplistic.

Wiesel has more questions than answers about the subject of hate. He wonders why victims of hate have not succeeded in transforming that hate into a warning, an alarm saying, "Look, look, hate means Auschwitz." Wiesel believes that every Jew should set apart a zone of healthy, virile hate, because, "whoever does not hate when he should does not deserve to love when he should."

In 1991 Wiesel was interviewed by Bill Moyers for a television special called *Facing Hate*. Moyers talked about the Russian prisoners at Buchenwald, who, when liberated, slaughtered the nearby German civilians simply for living beyond the barbed wire.

"Do you ever find yourself wishing that perhaps...it might have been better for you to have done what the Russian soldiers did?" Moyers asked.

"I never felt any attraction toward violence," Wiesel said. "I never tried to express myself through violence. Violence is a language. When language fails, violence becomes a language. I never had that feeling. Language failed me very often, but then, the substitute for me was silence, but not violence. It doesn't mean I'm proud of it. I'm not. It's simply my nature...." Wiesel said that he could not condemn the Russians and characteristically his answer becomes a question. "Who am I to judge?" he asked.

"When are we most truly human?" Moyers wondered later in the show. Wiesel answered this with the declaration that has shaped his life: "When we are weak and when we try to overcome weakness by not choosing inhumanity." He has also said, "There are all the reasons in the world not to have faith in humankind. In spite of that, I must have faith. I tell stories, I teach, I write books, because I have faith or must have faith in the reader, the student, the interviewer, or the therapist. It is a leap of faith. I have to believe that I can contribute to their becoming better."

Max Cleland

The truth comes into this world with two faces. One is sad with suffering, and the other laughs; but it is the same face, laughing or weeping. When people are already in despair, maybe the laughing face is better for them; and when they feel too good and are sure of being safe, maybe the weeping face is better for them to see.
— Elie Wiesel

And they laugh. They laugh with such despair that in the end, they will understand that there must be a link between the voice and the call, between man and his road, in the end they will understand that their feeling of despair is not absurd, for it may be the link that binds them to the king.
— John Neihardt

During the Vietnam war, Max Cleland was severely injured, leaving him crippled for life. Despite terrible anguish and pain, he was determined to find peace so that he would not spend the rest of his life embittered by what had happened to him in the war. He did this by immersing himself in humor, an attitude that allowed him to rise above his suffering and to find new a perspective on life. The humorist accepts tragedy, but does not spend his life in grief and mourning; he does something about it. He takes his sadness and makes it sing.

Max Cleland's office is in Georgia's gold-domed capitol. The building's cupola is topped the symbols of freedom—

31

a statue of a woman holding a sword and a torch. The American and Georgian flags ripple in the wind in front of mammoth Corinthian columns that stand at the building's entrance. Inside, on the second floor, Max Cleland, Secretary of State—a triple amputee—moves in his wheelchair to the rhythm of his own oratory.

"I like General Patton's definition of success: 'how high you bounce back after you hit bottom,' he says. That incorporates a certain understanding that we are going to fail along the way."

Cleland knows about hitting bottom and bouncing back. While fighting in Vietnam, he lost both legs and part of one arm in a grenade explosion. As a result, he became severely depressed and suicidal. He was able, however, to fight his misery. In fact, he fought so hard and bounced back so high that he was able to eventually become a state senator—the youngest man ever to have the position in Georgia—and also during President Carter's administration, he became the head of the Veterans Administration.

Unquestionably he is a diplomat and statesman, yet he also presents an interesting folksy quality, a characteristic that has remained with him from a life of living in the rural hinterlands. He gesticulates wildly with his arms—his good one and his stump. His movements are surprisingly springy and there is no doubt that all this energy inside him will not be trapped just because his body is severely damaged.

At one end of his huge office, next to a royal-blue love seat, coffee and pastries have been set up. The office has rich dark woods, parquet floors, high-backed chairs, a grandfather clock and brass door handles, each inscribed with the State Seal of Georgia. The room is filled with awards, trophies and memorabilia from the Vietnam war. A plaque commemorates the 1986 Citizen of the Year Award that Cleland won along with Bob Hope and Congressman Claude Pepper. Under a photo of John F. Kennedy, there is the saying, "Would you hire a vet with a bad back?" An award from a veterans organization addressed to "Capt. Max" says, "You never live until you almost die." Another citation proclaims, "To those who fight for it, life has a flavor the protected never know."

Cleland wheels up to the small sofa and presses his hand onto the cushion. He then does a little flip to move his body out of the wheelchair and onto the sofa. "Let me give you the gospel according to Cleland," he says, while tucking his empty trouser legs underneath him, "In my own dealing with trauma, with life blowing up in your face, I've learned a couple or three things. The human mind, body and spirit can undergo an incredible amount of trauma given one thing: support.

"Now there's internal support, and there's support from outside. Internal support is a strong sense of personhood or self-worth, and a sense of purpose and values. Internal support is the cornerstone of survival.

"I recently saw the female lead of [the movie] *Children of a Lesser God* on a TV talk program. She was deaf and the interviewer said, 'You must have had parents who supported you.' She said, 'Yes, they supported me, but I also supported myself.' On the surface that sounds like a brash comment, but sometimes there isn't support and you have to support yourself.

"Attitudes are what's important. Henry Ford, the great industrialist, once said, 'Think your best, study your best, and have a goal for your best. Never be satisfied with less than your best, and in the long run things will work out for the best.' I can say that now, but when I was laying on a cot in Walter Reed Hospital in 1968 I couldn't believe it. I had prepared. I had believed and there I was laying on a cot in Walter Reed recovering from Vietnam and wondering what it was all about. I couldn't look back and say it all worked out for the best.

For a long time Cleland suffered constant flashbacks of the grenade explosion, only each time he remembered, he tried desperately to change the ending. When he jumped from the helicopter, he ran in a crouched position, able to clear its spinning blades. On the ground where the chopper had lifted off, he saw a grenade. "It must be mine," he thought, since grenades had fallen from his gear before. When he bent down to pick it up, it exploded.

When his body stopped convulsing and his eyes came back into focus, he looked at his hand; there was nothing left but a splintered bone that ended at his elbow. He fought nausea and tried to stand, but one leg and a knee were also missing. His other leg was a soggy mess of flesh and green fatigue cloth. His combat boot dangled from the smashed leg.

He tried to fight off the soft blackness of unconsciousness that threatened to engulf him as he was flown to a surgical hospital. As the anesthesia took over, he asked the doctors to please try to save his leg; when he woke up, he saw that they hadn't been able to.

On his trip back to the States, his emotions were like a roller coaster. One minute he looked at the blue sky and was thankful he was alive, able to see, breathe, feel and think. The next minute he sank into despair, knowing he would never be the man he once was. Before the explosion he had stood six feet two inches tall and had been an athlete.

Virtually everything in Vietnam had been disillusioning to Cleland. In base camp his biggest battle had been with insects, skin rashes and monsoon rains. Soon he realized how minor those irritations were compared to what was ahead of him. He learned that his brigade was going to be dropped in the middle of three North Vietnamese divisions, but at that point it was impossible to change his orders. It was horrifying and so meaningless. The climatic explosion at Khe Sanh, which occurred just before the end of his tour of duty was especially senseless. American soldiers were killed by American artillery. Cleland felt like just another casualty in a meaningless war.

His hopes of getting artificial limbs were dashed by a doctor who told him that because Cleland didn't have any knees, he wouldn't be able to get up if he were to fall down. This made Cleland realize that he couldn't re-enter society even remotely to how he had left it. Knowing he would be set apart from others, Cleland became severely depressed. "I was in such a deep depression, so down and discouraged. I felt very much like the young man who called a suicide hot line, and got put on hold. When they came back on the line they told him, 'We discussed your case, and we think you are doing the right thing.'"

Nonetheless, something deep within Cleland told him that even though he didn't see any way back, he'd better look for ways to get back on the right track. He figured he could either get better or stay bitter. Staying bitter didn't work, it only made him hurt worse. He decided that the answer was not to change life itself, but to change his circumstances. "We often stand and look so long and so regretfully at the door that has closed, we fail to see the opportunities brought by the door that opens ahead," he says.

"Sometimes when you are so discouraged, so down and out and bleeding, in that valley of life where you are suffering, it's hard to look back [later] and say that it all worked out for the best. Yet ending it all is not the answer either. How a person responds to what happens to him is the individual's choice.

Rather than staying in the shell he built around himself when he first entered Walter Reed Rehabilitation Hospital, Cleland gained strength from the relationships he made with other amputees in the ward they called the "Snake Pit." When Cleland first entered Walter Reed Hospital, he was isolated by self-pity and bitterness, but by reaching out to others, he became less overwhelmed by his own psychological pain. "No man walks alone," Cleland says, "and when I learned that, I felt I learned the secret of life."

"Some days," Cleland explains, "you get the bear, and some days the bear gets you. On those days when the bear gets you, when you are really wiped out, desperate and exhausted, when it's hard to look in the mirror and say 'I'm really wonderful,' that's when good loving friends mean the most. A minister friend of mine says, 'In the service of love, only broken hearts will do.' When you have a broken heart for the first time, you understand how the rest of the world feels. It's a humbling and terrifying experience.... No man walks alone, and as soon as I learned that, I felt I learned the secret of life."

During our discussion, in one minute he seemed both exhilarated and depressed; he laughed and tears welled up in his eyes as he said, "Self-pity, perched on our bedsteads like a gargoyle, was waiting to leap on us at any opportunity." The other amputees in the hospital helped him to fight it by teaching him to laugh rather than to cry.

Cleland recalls one friend at the hospital who lost an eye and a leg to shrapnel and whose face, while waiting for plastic surgery, was a mess. He would go into an act for the elderly ladies who pushed the orange juice carts. "Well, Ma'am," he dead-panned, "I know it sounds a bit strange, but I came in here one day for a dental checkup and got run over by a food cart."

Cleland began to see the value of humor as a tension reliever. He dreaded his parents' first visit, because he didn't know how they would react when they saw what had happened to him. When he saw them climbing the entrance steps, he yelled, "Well, look what's coming. Another march on Washington." Their nervous laughter broke the ice. Then, when his parents and an aide tried to take him for a drive, they couldn't figure out how to get him in the car. Cleland responded with a joke. "What's the matter? Don't any of you know which end to grab?"

"I had been a very humorless person, caught up with the war and my disability. I was a serious, ineffectual pain in the rear.... I realized there's nothing more boring and unexciting than someone on a white horse who knows he's right. Look at the John Hinckleys of this world, the people who can't shake their sense of mission. They are absolutely humorless and very tight. People who have a sense of humor have a perspective and a sense of humility. Humor is a way of looking at life, and we can learn to use it."

Cleland was also learning a new way to view physical

therapy. He began to see it as a way to prepare for success. "We must prepare for when we are asked to rise again," he advises, determined not to give up the way many he'd observed in rehabilitation had. "You see individuals who choose to not do their best. It's like a foreign country to them. They don't expect the best from themselves, but this is an attitude they had before the injury, before the hurt."

Before Cleland's wounds had healed and his arm stump had drained, he diligently exercised his two "legs" and his one almost nonexistent arm. "If you don't use it, you lose it," his physical therapist told him. On a gym mat he did pushups from a rolled towel inserted under each leg stump, and slowly, very slowly, his body began to adjust to its new shape and to adapt to the new demands that were being placed on it. The muscles he had that were left began developing and compensating for muscles that had been lost. As a result, Cleland became strong where he had been weak. Exercising helped him to focus his attention on what he did have rather than on what was missing. By overcoming these challenges, he focused more on what he could do rather that what he could not do.

He tells me that he felt as if his life was a perfect illustration of a line Ernest Hemingway wrote, "life breaks us all and afterward many are strong at the broken places." (Cleland titled his autobiography *Strong at the Broken Places*.) Finding symbols and meanings that were both personal and universal dislodged his struggle from feelings of isolation. He also felt as if he learned many lessons that would both help others and help him relate to others.

Seeing other amputees learn how to walk on artificial limbs was the main thing that convinced him that it was possible for him. "There's no substitute for seeing hope in the flesh. There is no way to overstate the impact of one person's life on another's. The moment I saw another double amputee walking, I knew I could do it. In an instant, my attitudes toward the possibilities of my life changed."

Cleland's biggest fear while he was in the Snake Pit was that he would not be able to fit into the outside world. The foreword of *Strong at the Broken Places* is from Dr. Ronald Glasser's *365 Days*, which describes children in Vietnam who had just been injured and were waiting to be admitted to a pediatric clinic. "They were worried, every one of them, not about the big things, not about survival, but how they would explain away the lost legs or the weakness of their right arm. Would they embarrass their families? Would they be able to make it at parties with guys who were whole? Could they go to the beach and would their scars darken in the sun and offend the girls? Would they be able to get special cars? Above all, and underlying all their cares, would anybody love them when they got back?"

Cleland was hesitant to attend his first social event as a triple amputee, but his friends in the Snake Pit told him in so many words that they'd wipe the floor with him if he didn't go. It was an open house at a nurse's apartment, and Cleland wasn't given the time to turn down the invitation. Three men just picked him up from the hospital, gave him a borrowed sports coat and dumped him in a car. When they arrived, he said he felt like a wallflower sitting in his wheelchair amid the hubbub of party conversation. He couldn't shake hands and hold his glass at the same time, so he left the glass by the punch bowl, wheeled around the room to meet people, then returned to it.

To his astonishment, a lady came up and said she wanted to tell him her problems. "That did the whole thing 180 degrees." Cleland explains, "Not only was she not concerned about me, she thought I could help her. When you are visibly injured, people tell you their problems. It's funny, an uncanny phenomenon—like the ice is broken so they can level with you, and they come forth with things they wouldn't tell another soul. It was also a surprise to me to learn I had something to offer, that I could be of help to people who had been broken in different ways.

"I'm humbled and honored by that now, but back then it was an important turning point. When you're hurt," Cleland points out, "you think everybody is looking at you. Having a missing limb—even one—is very eye-catching. But missing three draws stares everywhere you go. Little four-year-olds just blurt out [their surprise] and I've learned to live with that.

"It was important for me to realize that everyone wasn't thinking about it. Even when you have something only temporary, like a pimple or a missing tooth, you think, 'Gawd, they're all goin' to see.' But the truth is that people don't care. That takes a lot of pressure off you, you know."

Hope started to come back. He invited a woman he'd dated before Vietnam to come visit him in Washington. Darlene knew what had happened to him and was still enthusiastic about spending the weekend with him. Since he had spent so little money when he was overseas, by then he had saved quite a lot. He reserved the largest suite in the Washington Hilton with a room for her and one for himself.

When he left the "Pit" that weekend, the other men whooped and shouted their encouragement to him. While waiting for his date to arrive, he pretended to read a magazine while keeping an eye glued to the hotel entrance. Darlene arrived just on time, and he wheeled up and greeted her. A bellhop carried her suitcase to the suite. They spent 20 minutes catching up and then suddenly, the conversation grew tense. She looked at her watch and exclaimed, "Oh, my God! My plane is leaving at 4:30 this afternoon. I must be going."

He was in shock at he watched her stand and walk to her suitcase. "Uh, can I help you?" he finally stammered foolishly.

"Oh, no, I can handle it," she said with a forced smile, "It's been nice seeing you, Max. Bye."

After she left, Cleland stared at the door a long time.

Then he wheeled himself to the elevator, went down to the bar and consumed several whiskey sours. At dinner, he tried to date all of the waitresses and by midnight he had even tried to date the cashier. They all responded to his requests with laughter and this embarrassed him even more. When he finally made his way upstairs, his stumps ached from the alcohol, and he tumbled into bed in the empty suite muttering, "The hell with it."

Still, Cleland did not give up. He invited yet another old girlfriend to come see him, and he was determined to have a good time. He offered to show her Washington's sights and buy her lunch. They took a cab to Lafayette Park across from the White House, and she pushed his chair since they had several blocks to go.

"It's good to see you, Max," she said.

"What there is of me," he tried to laugh.

"No," she objected softly, "you're all there, the Max I knew."

He reached over his shoulder and squeezed her hand. They approached a corner, and the wheels of his chair dropped off the curb. He was thrown into the gutter of Pennsylvania Avenue. In the dirt and cigarette butts, he scrambled about. One-armed and legless, he felt like a fish flopping on the shore. He couldn't bear to look at the woman with whom he'd been talking so confidently only minutes before. Suddenly a car turned and nearly hit him. He screamed. Two men rushed up and lifted him back into his chair.

His friend cried hysterically, saying she was sorry over and over while trying to brush the dirt from his empty trouser legs. He tried to comfort her as the crowd of curious onlookers broke up and drifted away. They hailed another cab which took them to the restaurant, but Cleland couldn't enjoy lunch. The shame of his fall still burned. He wondered what kind of a life was left for him. He wondered if he would be hauled around, as he put it, "like a sack of grain" for the rest of his life.

When he went home to Georgia for a visit, he was given a hero's welcome. A motorcade escorted Max and his parents from the Atlanta airport to Lithonia, where a giant fluttering banner reading "Welcome Home, Max" was suspended across the street. His old high school band was playing the "Star Spangled Banner," but when Max got out of the car, he felt embarrassed that he was returning in a wheelchair and that he only had one hand.

The hero's welcome did not make him feel like one. The first thing he asked his mother to do was to take down the Soldier's Medal and Silver Star certificates, because he felt that they had only been given to him out of compassion.

Cleland tried desperately to get back into his old life style. He visited popular nightclubs in downtown Atlanta with his friends, but the music was hard rock and it seemed too loud and explosive to him. Also, the band leader kept introducing Max to the crowd, first as the winner of the Purple Heart, then as the winner of the Congressional Medal of Honor. This caused everyone to turn and look at him; this was unsettling because, if anything, Max was trying to fit in, not stand out. As he watched the couples on the dance floor, he began to feel sorry for himself. The more drinks he had, the more melancholy he became. He began to feel ridiculous at a dance club in a wheelchair. This marked the beginning of a cycle of self-pity, heavy drinking and depression for Max.

Eventually he realized that he had changed too much to fit into his old life style and that he had to establish a whole new set of attitudes by which to live. Cleland soon discovered that growth is rarely pleasant or serene, and that deepening and extending oneself, especially into unfamiliar territory, is far from a tranquil endeavor.

"When one door closes another door always opens, but we often stand and look so long and so regretfully at the door that has closed, we fail to see the door that has opened. I began to have a restoration of mental health, to feel a newness of life when I entertained the possibility that doors might again open for me."

Cleland's biggest dream was to walk on the lifelike flesh-colored legs he'd seen other amputees wear. His

doctors told him that he would have to start with "stubbies"—balsa wood trainers that fit his stumps like a set of
holsters. In them, he only stood four feet tall. Instead of
shoes, he had to wear wooden rockers so he wouldn't fall
backward. At first, the "stubbies" felt torturous, but as
soon he was able to stand up, he was able to tolerate the
agony and started showing off by waddling around the
hospital. By the time the "stubbies" were removed, his
stumps were on fire.

He remembers feeling just like a toy he'd had as a
child, a little wooden soldier with stiff legs who wobbled
on a sloping board in jerking steps. Even though he may
have moved with jerking steps, he was moving and that's
all that mattered. From that point on he was ablaze with
pride and joy and felt that he could accomplish anything
he wanted to do.

Before Cleland was fitted for permanent, longer,
more realistic legs, he was discharged from the Army and
sent to the Veterans Administration Hospital. This, he
remembers, felt like a move to "an old elephant burial
ground." Mostly older veterans populated the hospital,
and at first he resented that they were able to walk
around in bathrobes and that they could simply take
drugs and pills to combat their pains and problems,
whereas he had to directly confront his problems with
hard work, pain and intense perseverance. That, he says,
was before he realized that the deepest wounds were
sometimes those that are not visible.

When Cleland was identified at the VA by a claim
number, not a name, he wondered how much more he
could take. Then he learned that he was going to get
his own apartment and this gave him an exhilarating
sense of independence and dignity—feelings he was
essentially robbed of by his experience in Vietnam and
his resulting injury. Taking a cab back and forth daily
to the VA for physical therapy made him feel more and
more independent.

Still dreaming of walking on human-like legs, Cleland pressured his rehabilitation supervisor to set up

conferences with limb-making firms. Of the three representatives who examined him, two said that they could not help him and that he would never walk again. The third said he would take the risk of fitting Cleland with limbs.

His cost-conscious supervisor ordered a set of old-fashioned wooden limbs instead of the more modern plastic ones that have hydraulic knees. When Cleland saw the order, he was frustrated, but took it as a message that, if he was ever going to walk again, it would be in the toughest way possible. He learned to walk on the gross-looking wood, putty and steel legs by suspending himself from parallel bars.

Fourteen months after losing his real legs, with his wooden legs, he was finally able to walk across the lawn of his home in Georgia. He would never again feel the grass under his feet and between his toes, but he had beaten the odds and had accomplished what so many had told him could not be done.

In December 1969 he was asked to testify at a hearing that was determining how the VA was treating the veterans who were returning from Vietnam. The hearing was well publicized and he was subsequently asked to speak at various organizations and churches. Talking to groups about the war and government rekindled the interest he had in politics. He decided that he wanted to play some role in government and decided to run for the state senate.

Not surprisingly, organizing and operating a campaign without legs proved to be an extremely difficult endeavor. Cleland hobbled along the sidewalks on crutches and when climbing stairs, he had to stop and rest after every third step. Frequently the ends of his stumps bled, but he felt that putting his best foot forward meant just that—even if it was plastic.

All the effort and campaigning paid off; he won the election. He was determined to wear his limbs to the victory party, because he wanted to be "on his feet." As he struggled up the stairs, the wife of the Lithonia mayor, who knew about the pain his artificial limbs were causing him, said, "Why are you wearing those? We love you just the way you are."

Later Cleland realized that this woman had given him important advice: he needed to love himself the way he was. His challenge was not to better himself in others' eyes, but to love himself the way he was. Except for one time when he was part of a friend's wedding, he never wore the limbs again.

"Sometimes I still dream about myself with legs, about running and shooting a basketball," his voice dwindling off as a shadow seemed to cross over his face. "Yet reality dawns. You run the sequence of events back, but the ending still doesn't change. That's rough sometimes, but it doesn't do any good to feel sorry for yourself or to be bitter."

In his first term as senator, Cleland worked on a resolution to negotiate a withdrawal from Vietnam which passed both houses of the Georgia legislature. In his second term, he worked closely with Governor Jimmy Carter, who was deeply committed to helping the returning Vietnam veterans and to making public places more accessible to the handicapped. Cleland was impressed by Carter, he says, because he seemed to follow an inner light that enabled him to take surprising risks.

In 1974 Cleland ran for lieutenant governor. Competing against ten political hopefuls, he knew it was a long shot, but so was everything else he'd attempted since the grenade explosion. When he lost the election, it was a strangely shattering experience. "Losing my legs and an arm had been an accident, I reasoned, but losing in my chosen field was a personal humiliating failure. My identity and self-esteem were wrapped up in politics. With defeat, my psyche careened down into a dark hole."

Struggling to escape his depression, he traveled through California campaigning for Senator Alan Cranston's re-election. One of the senator's aides informed him of an opening on the senate veterans affairs committee. Cleland applied and was hired for the job, which involved making on-site studies of VA hospitals.

As he drove to Washington, he began questioning what he was searching for. Himself? Some impossible dream? Excitement? Fame? Power? Although he had learned to accept his disability, he still wasn't happy with his life. He remembered an interview he'd read in the newspaper only a few months before. The subject, who'd just been assigned an important job, announced that he was going to "Let go and let God."

"I had never let go of anything I wanted in my whole life," Cleland says. "Instead, I wanted to be in control of everything. That's why those five words had so startled me when I first read them. How could one 'let go and let God' and still be successful? I realized that maybe this was faith—not a clutching, but a letting go; I certainly had never had that kind of faith in God." Cleland decided he needed the kind of inner light he'd seen in Jimmy Carter and that he needed and wanted God in his life.

After Carter was elected president, in a meeting at the White House, Cleland was asked to be head of the Veterans Administration. As he left the West Wing, he looked across the White House lawn toward Pennsylvania Avenue near the gutter where he'd accidentally fallen while he was on a date. Max Cleland has come a long, long way.

"There are two kinds of people in the world," Cleland says. There are those who believe and those who don't. People who believe in themselves and their goals get up in the morning differently than those who don't. It has to do with faith.... The reward of faith is seeing that in which you have believed. If you want to see anything in which you believe, you gotta exercise faith or else you won't take the steps of preparation. Now, I can believe the worst about myself anytime I choose, because quite frankly, I know the worst about myself. You can believe the worst about you, your business, this country, even life itself if you want. That's your choice. But you can believe the best as well. That's an exercise in faith. The great psychologist William James put it this way, 'Believe that life is worth living, and your belief will help create the fact.'"

Cleland declines to state what his future political ambitions might be. "On my best days I'm able to 'Let go and let God,'" he says. If it weren't for the grenade explosion, which he calls "The Great Death," Cleland does not feel he would have gone into politics, nor does he feel he would be the man he is today. When meeting new people, Cleland sometimes hands out autographed copies of the following prayer, written by an unknown Confederate soldier:

> I asked God for strength, that I might achieve.
> I was made weak, that I might learn humbly to obey.
> I asked for health, that I might do greater things.
> I was given infirmity that I might do better things.
> I asked for riches, that I might be happy.
> I was given poverty, that I might be wise.
> I asked for power, that I might have the praise of men.
> I was given weakness, that I might feel the need of
>   God.
> I asked for all things, that I might enjoy life.
> I was given life, that I might enjoy all things.
> I got nothing that I asked for—but everything
>   I hoped for.
> Almost despite myself, my unspoken prayers were
>   answered.
> I am among all men, most richly blessed.

In addition to faith, laughter too is a powerful force. Max Cleland feels he was blessed by learning to look at life with a bit of humor. "But, I've had good teachers," he says. "God has a sense of humor; if he didn't, he couldn't have made me."

By using humor, deep levels of Cleland's psyche were

able to mesh with his new situation. Humor also helped Cleland confront and work through his psychological pain in a way that did not overwhelm him.

Max Cleland treasures the healing value of humor, but he has also overcome his "Great Death" in other ways. He realized that he had to take life on its own terms and that meant accepting catastrophe and hardship as part of life's package. In other words, if he were to live in this world, he couldn't expect life to conform to his ideal. He embraced life, including all its absurdities and frustrations, and accepted the hardships as part of the challenge. Cleland did not avoid his problems or soften the pain they caused by directing his attention elsewhere; by facing his problems head-on, he deepened his immersion in life and this greatly strengthened him.

In war Cleland found horror, but he struggled against his inner darkness by counteracting futility with images of hope and grace, images that were not born out of sentimental and fuzzy superficialities, but from a deep engagement in life that has given him a deep understanding of universal truths.

Mike Wallace

The same week I interviewed Mike Wallace, he was on *60 Minutes* interviewing President and Mrs. Reagan. As Reagan's term of office was nearing its end, the couple would soon be leaving the White House. It was a familiar scene: Wallace shooting disarming questions at a world-famous leader.

Wallace's face and manner—the raised eyebrows signifying moral vigilance, the dark and penetrating eyes and pursed lips, perhaps implying skepticism—a mixture of sympathy and confrontation—has made him the most feared journalist in America.

When conducting an interview, Wallace's approach is to confront his subjects with some of the worst in themselves, with the assumption that how they handle it will illuminate the person behind their public persona. When Reagan was running for president, for example, Wallace asked him why people had described him as "actorish," a "dangerous hip-shooter," and a "light-weight." Since these same accusations were once also hurled at Wallace, he seemed to share some common ground with Reagan, so I listened carefully to the questions Wallace asked to see what, if anything, they might mirror about Wallace.

"In 1987, there was talk that you were really severely depressed, psychologically depressed," Wallace said. He then read a passage to Reagan from Martin Anderson's book *Revolution* about Reagan's reaction to the Iran/Contra affair: 'For the first time in his life, his credibility was challenged and soon the majority of the American people were convinced he had lied to them. His honor and integrity were on the line, and the public's doubts seemed to seriously depress him.'"

Integrity interests Wallace especially because back in the '50s, he made promises to himself that he never was able to keep. He vowed to concentrate on journalism and work in a field that gave him a sense of fulfillment, but he kept getting side-tracked by the lure of easy money that other jobs offered.

At a time when many other prominent newsmen were actively avoiding product endorsements, Wallace was a highly visible spokesman for Parliament cigarettes, a product whose use was suspected to be a cause of cancer. In addition, he once did commercials shortening called Fluffo. He also interviewed celebrities—interviews that involved little more than providing actors with a forum to plug their latest movies. Commercials and Hollywood hype were not the kind of work Wallace enjoyed, but it was lucrative and he told himself that because he had kids to support, he had to do it.

In 1962, when he was grieving over the death of his son Peter, Wallace was able to view his life from a larger perspective. He was able to differentiate between what was important to his life from what was not. Thrown onto new territory by the shock of the death of his son, he was able to face the important fundamentals of his existence, realizing that he had been transgressing against his own destiny. After his son's death, Wallace was finally able to take a long, hard look at himself—a process that allowed him to come to grips with his own faults. Now he sometimes confronts other people with their faults.

In 1962, Peter had just finished his second year at Yale and as a reward for his academic achievement, his father gave him a summer trip to Europe. That same summer Mike and his former wife Lorraine went on a tour of various foreign capitals for Westinghouse. When they returned home to New York, they were surprised that there were no cards or letters from Peter. Especially because his son always wrote every week, Wallace was extremely concerned. He contacted Peter's mother, Kappy, whom he'd married after they had been students together at the University of Michigan. She told him that the last letter she'd received from Peter reported that he had just left France and was planning to meet some friends in a Greek town on the Gulf of Corinth.

After another week went by without word from his son, Wallace became unbearably worried, so he flew to Greece to see if he could find him. Once he got there, he contacted the American Embassy in Athens and a consular officer helped him trace Peter's travels to the village of Camari. There they discovered Peter's baggage in a youth hostel, but Peter was nowhere to be found. Wallace walked through the town soliciting information until he found someone who, two or three weeks before, had seen a young American starting his way up a small mountain where he planned to visit a monastery.

In the hot summer sun, Wallace and the man from the embassy rode donkey-back up the mountain trail. After climbing for about three hours, they came upon a narrow ledge that appeared to have been partially broken off. It looked as if someone had slipped and fallen. Wallace looked over the ledge. About 75 feet down he saw Peter's dead body, shattered, broken and decomposed. From the way the ledge had separated from the mountain, it looked as if Peter may have been looking out at the gulf when the ground suddenly crumbled beneath him, throwing him over the edge.

Although Wallace was in a state of shock and emotionally wasted, he had to ride the donkey back into town to get help to retrieve his son's body and to bring it down from the mountain. He also had to hire someone to build a casket. It was dark by the time they were finished, and as he rode in a truck behind the vehicle that carried his son's casket, he felt a terrible loneliness. He looked up at the stars and they seemed to fill him with an uncanny sense of dread. Peter's death was so senseless, he wasn't sure if he could ever come to terms with it.

After bringing Peter's body down from the mountain, Wallace flew back to the States where he joined his wife Lorraine, Peter's mother Kappy, and his other son Chris Wallace, one of Peter's stepbrothers. Together they flew to Greece to bury Peter. "Pete had wanted to go to Greece since he was a kid," Wallace explains. "He used to dress up in sheets, like togas, make swords out of wood and shields from garbage can covers, so Kappy, his mother and I decided to bury him in Greece. We built a little wrought-iron fence around his grave."

Wallace feels that the funeral in Greece brought him closer to his son Chris. "We had not been very close because his mother and I had been divorced a long, long time." After the period of time that father and son spent together in Greece, "Chris understood me better and he knew I needed him more then."

The psychological pain of Peter's death was so intense for Wallace that he could barely speak about it. Even now, as we are speaking—years after his son's death—he gropes for words to describe his feelings. Finally, after trailing off into silence, he says, "You can just imagine. It was the worst thing that ever happened to me."

Peter had wanted to become a journalist like his father and Wallace regrets not having been a better example to him. "Peter had worked with me at Channel 13 as a copy boy, and he wanted to grow up and do what his brother Chris eventually did—become a writer and reporter. I was so utterly devastated by Peter's death—especially finding him the way I did—that during that awful time, I simply said, 'Hey, let's make a virtue of this tragedy. In effect, let's honor Pete by doing what I know he would have wanted me to do.'" It became very important for Wallace to become the kind of person Chris would have admired.

"Somehow, it grew inside me, a determination to make sense out of the senselessness of it all. Now when

I talk about it or write about it, it sounds to me a little pat, but it sure as hell was not. I can't say that it was a thunderstruck revelation that suddenly occurred to me; it just happened. I was talking and talking to Lorraine and trying to understand myself. This was obviously the worst thing that ever happened to me. There's no other way to put it.

"By this time, I had been married to Lorraine since 1955 and she had been nudging me gently but firmly to do work that I would find more fulfilling. And for a while I did, but then I guess I back-slid, because there was reasonably easy money doing other things."

Friends also encouraged Wallace to do something more worthwhile. "There was a man, name of Arthur Goldsmith, an older man of some means. He lived at the Waldorf Towers, an old bachelor whom we'd met at a dinner party. We liked him and he liked us, so we began to have dinner together at the Oak Room at the Plaza Hotel. He used to say, 'You are wasting yourself. You are capable of more. You are better than what you are doing.' I remember saying, 'I'm too old. I'm too far along. Come on. I'm in my late thirties. Time has passed me by to make these kinds of changes. I'm doing all right. I'm having a good time. I'm enjoying myself.' He'd say, 'You could be more useful doing something else.' I always had excuses for not doing it, somehow. It was always that I had kids to support."

After Peter's death, all the excuses Wallace made no longer mattered. Wallace had spent an uncomfortable year on a lightweight talk show, *PM East,* so a sense of not being in harmony with the best aspects of himself was fresh in his mind. "You start out to do what you think you want to do, and money gets in the way sometimes."

The way that Wallace coped with Peter's death—taking his own life goals more seriously and throwing himself into a more determined career path—still did not directly deal with the horrible pain of his son's death.

Later, at another difficult time in Wallace's life—during the trial of General William Westmoreland, when

Wallace's integrity was challenged—he again became very depressed, causing him to confront more directly the senselessness of his son's death.

We pace ourselves through losses and sometimes let in just enough pain so that we continue to function. Honoring Peter by becoming the kind of journalist he would have admired was a way for Wallace to continue to function while adjusting to the terrible loss.

As a broadcasting jack-of-all-trades who had tried a bit of everything, Wallace knew what he wanted to do with his life. In 1939, fresh out of the University of Michigan, he was hired as a radio announcer first in Grand Rapids, then in Detroit at station WXYZ where he first broadcast to a national audience. He narrated such classics as *The Green Hornet* and *The Lone Ranger*. He also broadcast the news. His show began with the rumbling sound of a fighter plane at full throttle. This was in the era when news was a "rip and read" operation; in other words, the announcer read what had been prepared by the United Press and the Associated Press.

In 1941 he moved to Chicago where he worked on a program called *The Air Edition of the Chicago Sun*. There he was encouraged to develop his own reporting and writing skills. In addition to establishing credentials in journalism, he began interviewing celebrities who were in town to plug their movies, TV programs and books. These glib exchanges do not compare with Wallace's later intense probing-of-the-person-behind-the-mask style of interviewing, but he did begin to sense that he had an aptitude for spontaneous reporting.

At the time, many journalists dabbled in entertainment. For example, Walter Cronkite emceed a variety show and played straight man to a lion puppet named Charlemane. Despite such activities, Cronkite was known primarily as a journalist, while Mike Wallace was known more as a personality. Even after he attained credibility as a first-class journalist, his reputation still carried the stigma of "entertainer."

One of Wallace's talk shows was called *Famous Names*. It was there that he met his second wife, actress Buff Cobb. In addition to celebrity talk shows, Wallace tried his hand at Broadway. In 1954, he played an idealistic art dealer in a Harry Kurnitz comedy called "Reclining Figure," but he didn't enjoy doing the same performance over and over again, nor did he especially like other aspects of working in theater.

In 1955, during a period of sadness and loose ends following his divorce from Buff Cobb, Wallace decided that he had spread himself too thin. As he and co-author Gary Gates write in *Close Encounters*, Wallace realized that he was "six characters in search of an identity." He vowed to concentrate his future on journalism.

That same year, Wallace was hired to anchor the Channel 5 news in New York City. Instead of airing two newscasts a night, at 7:00 and 11:00, news director Ted Yates suggested making the later show more provocative, designed to stimulate controversy. Wallace describes Yates, who had once broken his back when thrown from a bronco at a Cheyenne rodeo, as "a kind of cowboy in everything he did. I don't think he understood fear the way the rest of us do."

ABC's *Night Beat* went on live at 11:00 p.m. The set design was radical. "It was not the traditional and cheerful living room set, with the standard soft lights, the comfortable sofa and fake flowers. Instead, our studio was stark, pitch black except for the klieg light glaring over my shoulder into the guest's eyes and psyche."

Wallace says that the whole *Night Beat* staff was euphoric whenever they plotted how to nail a particular pompous blowhard or a fatuous egotist who was going to be on the show. "Our guests would be thoroughly, painstakingly researched and then once we got them on the air, I'd go at them as hard as I could. If they appeared to be hiding behind evasive answers, I'd press them or cajole them to knock it off and to come clean. If, in response to pressure they became embarrassed or irritated or sullen, I'd try to exploit that mood instead of retreating into a tone of amiable reassurance. Oversimplified, that was the formula we had in mind: candor—ours and theirs—with enough time to draw them out."

Night Beat had bite, edge and zest. Wallace was excited by the unpredictability of the show and discovered that if the questions were provocative enough, even pallid answers revealed character. One guest, Mike Quill, head of the Transport Workers Union, said he resented being asked if he was a religious man, perhaps because during the McCarthy era he'd been called "Red Mike." Quill said it was a "lowdown question," and wagging his finger and shouting, he proclaimed the program to be nothing but "a peep show."

In one interview, Wallace asked a New York fashion designer, Mr. John: "Since it is common knowledge that homosexuals make up a large part of the fashion field, isn't it true that an unconscious hatred of women—so typical of homosexuals—had been the force responsible for the dress absurdities of recent years?" Wallace admits he went too far when he interviewed Al Capp, the cartoonist who created the comic strip "Li'l Abner." Capp loved saying outrageous and antagonistic things, and after each acid comment, he would giggle. Wallace confronted Capp about his "compulsive" laugh, and this unnerved Capp. Wallace, fully aware of the effect he was having, persisted until Capp's face broke out in a sweat and his body began to shake. Later Wallace admitted that it was a callous thing to do, as "indefensible as sticking pins in a butterfly."

In a colorful interview, ex-mobster Micky Cohen admitted that he had killed people, but only those who "deserved to be killed." While discussing his bookmaking operation, he commented that various politicians had been bribed. When he began to get specific about which politicians he felt were dishonest, Wallace did not retreat; he would never have imagined that Cohen would say anything about specific people without the hard evidence that would provide proof. Instead, when Wallace asked for clarification, he got a torrent of reckless slander.

Cohen focused on Los Angeles police chief William Parker, who he called a thief, an alcoholic and a sadistic degenerate. Later Wallace realized he should have dissociated himself from the statements unless they could be proved. Parker filed suit and ABC's insurance company ended up having to pay him, settling out of court for a large sum.

Another imbroglio involved Washington columnist Drew Pearson, who said that because the book *Profiles in Courage* had been ghostwritten, it was dishonorable for John F. Kennedy to accept a Pulitzer Prize for it. Threatened with another libel suit, the ABC brass offered an official apology.

When Wallace was originally hired by ABC, news director and anchorman John Daly had not been consulted. In Dally's opinion Wallace was not a "real" journalist, only an interviewer, and the legal action that resulted from Wallace's interviews gave Daly fodder for his complaints.

Wallace knew that as long as Daly was at ABC, he would not have much of a future there, so he welcomed the move of *The Mike Wallace Interview* to Channel 13 in 1959. Wallace felt that his stint at ABC had hurt him in some ways because reviewers who had previously commended him for his candor changed their opinion and now saw him as "a reckless hip-shooter." He knew, too, that certain TV executives viewed him as a headline-seeking troublemaker.

During the two years that he was with Channel 13, Wallace moonlighted for the tobacco company, Philip Morris, an association which may have undermined his solid achievements in journalism. For his first year at ABC, Philip Morris was the sponsor of *The Mike Wallace Interview*. After they dropped the program, Wallace remained friends with the company's president, Joseph Cullman; Wallace later became a prominent spokesman for the tobacco giant. Unfortunately, this hurt Wallace in various ways. In 1960, when he worked with David Wolper on a documentary called *The Race for Space*, the networks would not buy it; as one executive told Wolper,

"We wouldn't want the man who measures the quarter-inch filter on a Parliament cigarette measuring the missile gap between the Soviets and the Americans."

When *The Mike Wallace Interview* went off the air for good in April 1961, Wallace received an offer to co-host *PM East*. He was not comfortable with the program because it seemed similar to entertainment shows he'd done earlier, but since he did not feel confident that he would get a better offer, he accepted a one-year contract, despite the disquieting feeling that he was "locking himself into the wrong kind of vehicle."

From the beginning in June 1961, Wallace wallowed in embarrassment. He felt that his personality was too intense, too heavy for the "gush and prattle routine" of *PM East*. When he tried to inject flashes of the old *Night Beat* fire into the "happy-talk" atmosphere, it backfired. In one interview when he asked Burt Lancaster about his alleged bad temper, Lancaster accused Wallace of being "self-consciously sensational" and with that, walked off the show. Viewers familiar with Wallace's serious work wondered what he was doing in this "buck and wing" stint.

After Peter's death, Wallace realized how excruciatingly painful his performance had been and that he could no longer endure being part of this frivolous Hollywood hype. He realized that in order to move forward, he first had to shed those parts of himself he no longer liked. His first step was to give up the Parliament commercials and then he spread the word that he would no longer host any more game or talk shows.

After conversations with producers in which he talked himself out of more entertainment-like jobs, some of which offered as much as $150,000, Wallace consulted attorney Jerry Johnson, an old Navy pal who handled his finances. Wallace wanted to know how much money he had because he planned to take a year off to devote himself to news exclusively. Then he wrote letters to Dick Salant of CBS, Jim Hagerty of ABC and Bill McAndrews of NBC. "In effect," Wallace told me, "the letters said, 'I'm going to do this come what may. I'm going to sanitize myself. I have enough money saved to last a year, and I want to work for you.'" He acknowledged that his career had been a checkered one, but that now he wanted to work exclusively as a newsman.

Cordially, with polite messages and pleasant conversation, all three men turned him down because they said there were no openings. He was asked to host a game show, but rather than take a job that he felt was precisely where he did *not* want to be, Wallace chose to spend the entire fall and winter months unemployed. For a man who thrived on work, a person full of vitality who usually had several projects going at once, being unemployed was like a prison sentence. He spent long, vacant hours waiting for the phone to ring, but in spite of how miserable he was, he stuck to the commitment he had made to himself and to Peter. In February, Wallace got an offer to anchor the evening news in Los Angeles, and although it wasn't network television, he reasoned that if he put in a couple of good seasons in California, the networks might give him a chance. But before Wallace accepted the offer, he got a call from Dick Salant of CBS.

Salant was impressed with a rumor he'd heard that Wallace had offered to buy the Parliament cigarette commercials from Philip Morris. The story wasn't true (Joseph Cullman, president of Philip Morris, had offered to pull the commercials from the market), but it did represent Wallace's desire to distance himself from the cigarette commercials.

Salant told Wallace that at CBS he'd have to begin at a local station. Financially, Salant's offer was roughly one fourth of what Wallace would have made had he continued to do commercials and entertainment. But Wallace, who had already come to accept the monetary limitations that his choice of work imposed, was pleased.

His colleagues at CBS, however, were not as happy. When Wallace was picked to anchor the *CBS Morning News*, an in-house anti-Wallace faction surfaced. Among them was Harry Reasoner, who Wallace said looked at him "like I was a hair in his soup." Reasoner, who had many loyal long-time friends at CBS, was the host of a midmorning news and feature program called *Calendar* that was being pulled from the air to make room for the *CBS Morning News*. News writer Joan Snyder later confessed that they were all contemptuous of Wallace who they likened to a sleazy Madison Avenue pitchman.

Wallace responded by keeping a low profile and concentrating on doing an excellent job. Since he had done so many different kinds of programming over the years, he could draw on a wide variety of experiences and was able to project poise and an air of authority. Viewers were impressed, and eventually so too were his colleagues. In the spring of 1964, Harry Reasoner stretched out his hand and said, "Look, this is silly. I can't stay sore at a guy who's doing as good a job as you're doing. Let's be friends."

Wallace's relationship with his "amusing pal" Reasoner blossomed and in 1968 Don Hewitt, the creative force behind CBS News, suggested that they team up on an ambitious news feature program to be called *60 Minutes*. "You and Reasoner will be great together," Hewitt told him. "Harry will be the white hat and you'll wear the black hat." Wallace thought the title was pedestrian until he saw the ticking stopwatch motif. Gradually his reservations gave way to Hewitt's enthusiasm and he became excited about the idea, especially about the fact that he would be able to do more in-depth interviews.

Wallace never expected to see the day when a news broadcast would consistently challenge the most popular entertainment shows, but *60 Minutes* continues to do just that. He attributes its early popularity in part to Watergate and "a widespread perception of the press as a noble posse that went out after the outlaws and brought them to bay." He doesn't think that perception is particularly accurate. He acknowledges that journalists can become arrogant, self-righteous and "too willing to assume we are on the side of the angels and too ready to suspect the motives of those we scrutinize."

As the pioneer of the format of the candid and penetrating television interview, a watchdog in a free and open society, Wallace strikes a responsive chord with many Americans who are also outraged at kickback schemes, phony health clinics and diploma mills. Many people, when indignant about some aspect of institutions that should be changed, instead of contacting government agencies, write a letter to Mike Wallace. Best known for his browbeating interviews with both the famous and the infamous, his trademark—confronting people with the worst in themselves—works, because he has also confronted the worst in himself.

Mike Wallace is able to demand high moral standards of those whom he interviews because he was able, in the aftermath of tragedy, to begin to demand the same of himself. He turned an event that seemed so senseless— his son Peter's death—into an event of great positive meaning.

Indeed, it is as if Peter's death gave his father a task to master and a more determined conscience.

Anne Caput

Some people believe that this is a just and fair world. What happens when these people discover just how harsh reality is and just how much injustice exists in this world? Some people become aggressive at every perceived affront, but this only serves to fan their rage past containment or direction, and it is a lonely course. Others extinguish all feeling so as not to feel the rage, but this is a lifeless course.

Others, like Anne Caput, have learned to come to terms with the injustices in this world. She is still able to affirm a life for herself. She has learned to discriminate between the things she can do something about and those she cannot. She has learned when airing a grievance will make a positive difference and when to let it go.

Almost 13 years ago, Anne Caput, a nurse, was tried for murder because she was allegedly responsible for administering a fatal dose of morphine to a patient, Norma Leanues, who many believed had died from cancer. (The prosecutors tried to claim that it was the drug that killed her, not the cancer.) Caput did indeed administer the painkiller (as did all the other nurses who cared for her), but Caput claimed that she was simply following the instructions of a doctor who put in an order that the patient, who was in extreme pain, be made as comfortable as possible with unlimited amounts of morphine.

Today, she describes the ordeal of being on trial for murder: "It was so unbelievable and horrendous, like a nightmare, like I'm going to wake up and everything is going to be okay." As the legal system began to infiltrate and control her life, she saw what a dreadful and powerful machine it was. She was amazed at what little association the legal process had to truth or justice. Moreover, she believed that the trial was being fueled by the district attorney's political ambitions and also the hospital staff's need for someone other than themselves to take the rap. The doctor who Capute said had prescribed the morphine in unlimited amounts as well as the hospital administrators (who had full access to how much morphine the patient was receiving) were given immunity from prosecution for their testimony.

The newspapers sensationalized the case and described Capute and what had allegedly happened in a way that bore little resemblance to the truth. They called it a mercy killing. This was particularly implausible because of all the patients Capute had cared for, she had the least connection to Norma Leanues and therefore had no reason to have a special interest in her. In fact, Leanues was in so much pain that Anne had never even had a real conversation with her. She had never chatted with her about anything remotely intimate, yet after Leanues' death, the two women became closely intertwined. To Anne, this was a particularly "crazy twist."

Those with whom she did have real interaction—the colleagues with whom she worked—went along with the hospital's scapegoating and testified against her. Sadly, most of her close friendships with co-workers ended. Perhaps they really believed the hospital's allegations, perhaps they were just lining up with the stronger power (the hospital) or perhaps they were attempting to protect their jobs. For whatever reason, they all abandoned her. To make matters worse, her marriage became strained to the breaking point. Except for the support of her dedicated attorney, Pat Piscitelli, as well as his staff, Anne fought a lonely battle against huge and alien powers that could easily confine her to prison for a very long time.

Knowing she could not mentally survive prison, she decided that she had to take charge and have a say in her own fate. On the day the jury was to decide Capute's fate with their verdict, she brought a gun with her into the courtroom, hidden in her handbag. If she was found guilty she planned to stick the barrel of the gun in her mouth, cock the hammer back and pull the trigger. She felt that she had already been pushed around too much by too many people and she was determined that nobody was going to drag her out of the courtroom in chains. At that time she would have preferred to be taken out dead.

"Suicide is a cop-out," she says now, "but [at that time] I had to grasp at it because I was between a rock and a hard place. It was my only control left, the only control I had over my own destiny. It was my safety parachute. I figured, 'Either I'm going to get out of this period or I'm going to get out of this world.'"

As she sits at the kitchen table in the ranch home her husband built in Plympton, Massachusetts, she says, "I wouldn't have believed it at the time, but now I can say that the trial was the best thing that ever happened to me. There is no way I could have grown so much spiritually without it. I only wish life's lessons didn't have to be so hard, so hurtful."

She frowns for an instant then takes a drag on her cigarette. She lets the smoke out calmly and evenly and then her face, framed by pale blond hair, becomes soft again. There's an unflappable quality about her. It's as if she feels that because she was able to get through such an outrageously horrible ordeal, she can now get through anything that life throws at her.

The trial forced her onto unfamiliar ground where she had to extend herself in unfamiliar ways. The uncomfortable feelings—the fear, the anxiety, the shame, the hurt—called forth courage and wisdom and revealed strengths that she didn't know she possessed.

Gary Provost wrote a book about Capute's experience

entitled *Fatal Dosage*. Upon reading it, Anne noticed how the author portrays her as a woman who cried all the time. "This was a commercial book. Gary did a good job given it was written in six weeks, but it's not *War and Peace*. You can't expect a lot of depth, but it just wasn't true that I was crying all of the time. One of my defense mechanisms was never to cry. 'Don't show the bastards you are vulnerable.' That's where I was back then and where I can still drift back to now. Appearances were important to me then. If I cried, it was when I was alone."

As she looks back at her life before the murder charge, she feels that she lived in a daze, in which she spent too much time focusing on trivial things. But during the trial things changed dramatically. Since she had planned to kill herself if she was found guilty, she was literally fighting for her life and couldn't be bothered by what had interested her before. "I was on trial for murder and I just couldn't get too excited about the price of hamburger."

Now she views life as a continual tour de force. She knows that hard experiences instruct: "I'm still here, because I have more lessons to learn. My spot on the planet Earth is I'm a student in a classroom, and I have just scratched the surface of the lessons I have to learn."

Since the trial Capute has taken a serious spiritual look at herself and at life. Now she is more open about her feelings, more accepting of others and far less judgmental. "I was very inflexible before—there was no bending for this reed. And I used to push my way on others, mostly my children. Now I'm more accepting. I've been judged and it's scary, very scary. I've been there and I know I don't have the right to judge anyone."

Much of the work Capute has done on herself since the trial has focused on forgiving her husband, who was not supportive of her, and forgiving the colleagues who testified against her. To hold grudges is not the kind of life-sucking energy she wants to have inside herself.

On the back of a small cardboard bird that hangs in her kitchen are the words, Let it go. "Life is too short to hate anyone," she says. There were times when she never would have believed she could forgive those who made life so difficult for her, but events have changed her thinking a great deal.

She remembers the way the ordeal began: on May 22, 1980, when she was summoned to a meeting with four hospital administrators, Anne worried that she was in trouble because she had been caught pilfering pain medication for a nurses' aide who had an abscessed tooth.

She was relieved when they questioned her about a patient—Norma Leanues. Anne figured it was some minor infraction regarding forms which was far less serious than stealing medication. When asked about Norma Leanues' condition during the days preceding her death, Anne reported that Mrs. Leanues suffered terribly, cried out a lot and that she had tears constantly streaming down her face, that she would clutch at her chest and that she had a hard time swallowing.

Their questioning then changed tone; Capute was asked about the exact wording of the conversation she'd had with the doctor who had been in charge of Norma Leanues, Robert Hillier. "Give her anything she wants. Just make her comfortable," Anne quoted Dr. Hillier as saying. It was common hospital practice for doctors to give verbal orders.

She was asked why she had repeatedly given Mrs. Leanues 30 milligrams of morphine when the written order had only been for 15 milligrams. Anne answered that she had wanted to make the patient as comfortable as she could. Although she had just explained that this was the doctor's oral order, everyone in the room became uncomfortable and would not make eye contact with her. Anne was frightened when they asked her if she knew what the effects were of giving a person that amount of morphine.

"My God," Anne said, "it would be enough to kill an elephant."

At the end of the meeting, Anne was told that she

would be on administrative suspension for three days. Anne felt this was unfair since she had only been following the doctor's orders, but she figured it was a misunderstanding that would be cleared up as soon as Dr. Hillier returned from vacation.

When she told Charlie, her husband, about the suspension and that she had given the patient large doses of morphine on Dr. Hillier's orders, she expected him to be sympathetic, to say that he was sorry that such an unfair thing had happened to her. But Charlie just asked why she had done, in his words, such a stupid thing. He expressed some concern over her suspension because it meant three days without pay, then he rolled over and went back to sleep.

After the three days passed she was told that she still could not go back to work. Then an assistant nursing administrator called her and said, "Your interests and the hospital's interests have diverged. Get a lawyer."

Then she was indicted on charges that, expressed in formal legal terminology, said that she "did assault and beat one Norma C. Leanues with intent to murder her and by such assault and beating did kill and murder the said Norma Leanues." When she heard this she knew for certain that she wasn't going to wake up and find that things were okay. It may have seemed like a nightmare, but the experience of being fingerprinted and having mug shots taken made the situation dreadfully real.

Because Norma Leanues' death was viewed by many as a mercy killing, the newspapers had a field day with the case. Reporters hounded Anne. They shouted questions through the door of her home while she and her family hid inside. Anne couldn't figure out how her statement that she had given Mrs. Leanues enough morphine to kill an elephant had leaked to the press until she learned that the administrators and Dr. Hillier had been given immunity from prosecution in return for their testimony against her. Anne felt completely abandoned by people she'd respected.

The trial began on September 9, 1981 in Superior

Court in Fall River, Massachusetts—in the same granite courthouse where nearly a century before Lizzie Borden had been tried for the murder of her father and stepmother. To Anne the building felt like a huge stone monster that would consume her.

To counteract her feelings of helplessness, Anne decided that she had to take an active role in her defense. "I just couldn't sit back and let the world run over me or just let nature run its course." She spent every morning at Pat Piscitelli's office where she participated in planning the defense strategy and helped in the jury selection. She was even present when some of the prosecution witnesses came in to see the DA.

Piscitelli was one of the best criminal lawyers in the area and Anne had to mortgage her house in order to hire him. Piscitelli's defense for Capute was built on a system of concentric circles. His first point was to prove that Leanues died of cancer, not a morphine overdose. If the prosecution broke through that defense, he would try to prove that Leanues didn't die from the morphine that Anne had specifically given her; other nurses had also been giving the patient large doses of the drug. If the DA penetrated that ring, Piscitelli would try to prove that Anne was only following the doctor's orders. His last defense was Anne herself, a nurse who had done nothing more than act in the best interests of a patient.

When the proceedings started, the DA pointed to Capute and said, "That woman murdered Norma Leanues." One of the prosecution's most important witnesses, Dr. Robert Hillier, said that he had never issued a "no time limit" order for morphine and that he had never said to make the patient as comfortable as possible. He claimed that his order had been for 15 milligrams of morphine every three hours on an as-needed basis.

The DA then had Hillier read the nurses' reports which documented that doses of 30 and 45 milligrams had indeed been given to Leanues every two hours instead of every three. Anne Capute's initials were written

after many of the injection documentations, but other
nurses had also given large doses of morphine, as proved
by their initialing. Piscitelli substantiated that dozens of
people were aware or could have been aware of the
amount of narcotics that Norma Leanues had been receiving. Nursing supervisors were advised daily about
medications.

When Robert Hillier was on the stand, Piscitelli
attempted to bring out the man's haughtiness. When
questioned about nursing procedures, Hillier proved to
be extremely ignorant and gave the impression that he
couldn't be bothered by such unimportant things. Igno-
rance of this sort, Piscitelli argued, could lead to serious
mistakes in communication with the nursing staff.

Piscitelli had a volume of grand jury testimony on
the defense table. On several occasions, he strutted
across the room, picked up the volume and showed Hillier
contradicting what he had just said under oath on the
stand.

The most painful testimony for Anne was that of
Maureen Costello, her nursing supervisor, whom Anne
almost worshipped. Costello said that Anne had not
followed safe nursing practices, which sounded to Anne
as if she was criticizing her for not being a good nurse.
Anne was very hurt. She remembered that the quality of
her nursing performance had earned her a step and a
half pay raise just months before she was suspended.
And now her supervisor didn't think that she was a good
nurse?

The district attorney, Ron Pina, gazed away every
time Anne looked at him. Anne felt that if you are going
to accuse someone of murder, you ought to be able to look
them in the eye, so she was determined to make eye
contact with him. On the day she went to the hospital
with the jury, Anne got into the elevator with the judge
and Pina. With Pina trapped, she looked him straight in
the eye, winked and said, "Hi Ron." Ron seemed unnerved, his face turned red, and he started twitching.

The trial went on and on and on. In fact it was the

longest trial in the history of the county. Every night the evening news ran segments of the day's activities in court. Tired of the public's conceptions of her, Anne escaped the fishbowl she lived in by withdrawing into an inner compartment of her mind, safe from the scrutiny of the courts and the media.

"I didn't require a lot of sleep, not more than three or four hours. I would lose myself in music—Neil Diamond records mostly. It was relaxing and let me forget about what was going on. I could lose myself in it."

When Anne thought about what was happening to her, killing herself turned from a tentative idea to a deep black conviction. Since the days she had left with her family seemed numbered, she spent a lot of time with her daughters, who now stayed close to home. Before the trial, it had almost been impossible for the whole family to sit down to dinner together, but now the girls sensed that they might not have their mother around very long.

Even Barbara, the oldest daughter, came over after work. There had been long-standing tension between Barbara and her mother because Barbara was born when Anne was very young and was raised by her grandparents. Barbara felt Anne didn't care much about her. During the trial, however, she stuck by her mother. The crisis brought mother and daughter together and even helped them to repair the years of alienation.

As the day of the verdict neared, Anne gave away her prized possessions. She had never been very materialistic, but she cherished a collection of cut glass candy dishes, goblets and bowls, which had been handed down from her grandmother. When she divided this collection between her four daughters, they knew she was serious about killing herself if she was convicted.

Anne talked openly about her suicidal plans with Warren Magee, a close friend who was engaged to one of Anne's best friends. Since he was frequently depressed and often discussed taking his own life, Anne felt he would understand her feelings. But Warren didn't take the disclosure very calmly. His hands trembled, perhaps because similar feelings were so familiar and scary to him. He said when the time came, he would try to talk her out of it, but the time never came, because Warren took his own life before Anne's trial was over.

Warren walked into Anne's house while she was in court—the doors were never locked—and jimmied open the gun cabinet. Since he didn't know anything about guns, he jammed a .45 magnum shell into a .270 Enfield rifle, but it did the job. He shot himself in the temple and died instantly.

Anne's daughter, Lori, who had stayed home from school that day because of a bad sunburn, heard the shot. She rushed into the room where the cabinet was and found his body. After calling the police Lori became hysterical and by the time Anne got home she was almost catatonic. She sat cross-legged in the living room, mute, staring off into space. Anne's youngest daughter, Meredith, was so upset by what had happened that she refused to come home for two weeks.

Worrying about her daughters enabled Anne to shift the focus away from herself. Anne got Lori into therapy and eventually she was able to work through the catastrophe. Anne redecorated Meredith's room so that it looked entirely different and eventually Meredith was coaxed back into her room.

Anne also was supportive to her friend who had been engaged to Warren. "I'd get out of court and I'd run like hell to help them make funeral arrangements. It was a bizarre time, and it was fine to be busy. It sure as hell beat sitting around thinking about myself."

In addition to all of this, Anne's marriage was in trouble. She wanted Charlie to accompany her to court, to be sympathetic, but Charlie dealt with the stress of the trial by avoidance. He told Anne that he could best help the family by working at his job as a carpenter because it would help pay their debts. Anne resented this approach.

Reading was another way she kept from thinking about the mess her life was in. She needed a whole new set of answers to life's questions and began studying Taoism. "Two years earlier I would have said [what I was reading] was all crazy stuff, but then I would have thought that being tried for murder would have been crazy too.

"Taoism teaches you that society's rules are a crock of shit and you only need to conform to the laws of the universe. Taoism teaches you to live more simply and to get rid of the junk we carry around in our heads." She began to believe in reincarnation and began to see death as a kind of freedom, as a way of being out in the wilderness permanently.

Instead of groaning incessantly over the illegitimacy of the system, she found a philosophy that didn't believe in society's rules. Instead of hanging onto the rage she felt toward the huge amorphous "system," she turned away from it, working instead on her own inner development.

When the jury finally went out to deliberate, Anne did not have a sense of how she would be judged. The DA had a cancer specialist testify that Norma Leanues had not been terminally ill. He reasoned that because the cancer did not involve any vital organs it was not life-threatening. With treatment, he said, Leanues could have lived anywhere from another six months to several years. Anne's attorney also brought medical experts to the stand. They listed Leanues' combination of diseases and claimed that they alone could clearly have caused her death.

A surprise witness, Kathy Menard, a nurse at the hospital who had not come forward earlier, gave the trial a potentially damaging twist. She claimed that Anne's version of the conversation with Dr. Hillier was different than Anne had explained it.

Anne says, "She was on a totally different part of the floor of the hospital during the conversation. In the beginning I was wicked angry that this woman was coming out of nowhere and giving testimony that was totally a lie. In order to cope with it, I had to realize that this was not the first time this person had lied. I honestly believe that poor Kathy, and I have to say poor Kathy, came up with a way, in her mind, to be a star."

Piscitelli brought in a diagram of the hospital floor and showed that had Kathy actually overheard the conversation, she would have been 15 feet away, which is not near enough to be able to hear two people quietly talking. Occasionally the lawyer would press a hand in front of his mouth as if to suppress a laugh, because he didn't want the jury to take Kathy too seriously; he felt that it was preposterous for a nurse who had heard thousands of such conversations to come forth a year and a half later with a precise recollection of one of them. However, it was impossible for Anne or her lawyer to know what the jury made of Kathy's testimony.

At the end of the trial, Anne addressed the jury herself. She was terrified, but somewhere she summoned up the courage to say what she had to say. She talked about her past—the seven children she had raised and the several jobs she had had while pursuing her goal of becoming a nurse. She said she loved nursing and cared deeply about her patients. She also described Norma Leanues' agony and how the woman had cried out in pain.

"If you believe the district attorney when he says that I killed Norma Leanues," Anne declared, "I ask you to bring back a guilty verdict. But if not, if you believe what I swear to you is true—that I did nothing other than try to help Norma Leanues with her agony and her suffering—then set me free and return me to my family." Several members of the jury were in tears by the time she had finished.

Piscitelli told Anne that an innocent verdict would come back quickly, so when the jury did not come back the first night, Anne was sure they had lost. Late that night, after her family had gone to bed, Anne wrote a long letter to her daughters that explained her planned suicide in the courtroom.

"By now you have seen something horrible and your mind is full of questions. I can't answer them all. All I can tell you is that I love my freedom more than anything and I could not bear to be in prison. I would just shrivel up and die. If I have to die I want it to be my way. When Warren died, it seemed like the world was closing in on us and there was so much despair. But we survived. We were strong. All of you girls are strong and you will survive this."

At 12:55 the next day the jury filed in. The courtroom was packed with reporters, the Leanues family, employees of the hospital and curious onlookers. Anne sat up front at the defense table and clutched the pocketbook containing the gun to her chest. She was feeling crazy, but said to herself, "I'd have to be crazy not to be feeling kind of crazy right now."

The clerk faced the jury and said, "Ladies and gentlemen of the jury, have you reached a verdict?"

"We have," said the foreman. Piscitelli squeezed Anne's shoulder.

"On the charge of murder, how say ye?"

"Not guilty."

"After it was all over," Anne says, "I was angry at the outpouring of congratulations. My brother, who I haven't talked to for years and years and years, showed up here on Saturday morning with two goddamn plants of mums. I'll never forget it. All of a sudden, he says, 'My sister.'"

She wonders if he would have been as ready to proclaim her as his sister if she had lost. "This country is so into winning and competition. We all love a winner and no one knows what becomes of the loser."

Anne also had to deal with her anger over her husband's behavior. "He loved the limelight. He loved the photographers coming to the door. It was a whirlwind immediately after the trial. There were interviews and celebrations, and I didn't have time to sit back and contemplate how he had been reacting to a very threatening situation. Charlie wanted to come to New York to do the *Good Morning America* show with us, but I lied and said, 'No. You can't come.' " To herself, she thought, "You son of a bitch. You weren't there for me, and now you want to share the spotlight."

Anne's capacity for being more accepting and less judgmental did not come easily. "I had to keep leaving. Once I stepped back, which I did by going away for three or four weeks at a time, I contemplated Charlie's behavior. The more I could let myself understand that that's just who he is, the better I felt. He will change if he wants to, but I can't make him. Part of my growth has been to understand that that's who he is.

"I still have flares of anger. Charlie still slips. Last year he went to Florida to see an uncle he hadn't seen in 20 years. I had never met this uncle, but I met the aunt once and she ignored me. It was a horrible scene. So Charles goes down there and starts talking about the book and the movie. These people I've had no contact with for seven years call me up and ask me when the movie is coming out."

Anne no longer dwells on the past and has moved on with her life. She still gets angry when people try to put her into those media images, but she doesn't require hostility to feel authentic. She does not want to be known as the nurse who was tried for murder; there is so much more to her. She was extremely overweight at the beginning of her ordeal and since she was charged with murder she has lost 150 pounds and seems more fully to inhabit her own nature.

She likes herself more now and has been able to slowly "let go of my defense mechanisms." She has also rearranged her priorities. "I try to do things now without looking for the rewards and recognition."

"I used to try to save the world, but now I don't interfere. When my daughter Susan is in trouble, I do not run out to try and save her. I've learned that she has to make her own decisions and solve some of her own problems by herself. Otherwise, I might be hindering her growth. That's not to say that I've developed a 'You made your bed now lie in it attitude.' I'm still there for guidance."

Since the trial, Anne has dedicated her career to

helping the terminally ill. "They give you more than you give them. Terminal people don't care about the material world and the shit that goes with it. They tend not to be judgmental and don't carry the jealousies, angers and hates that many of us have. They have taught me to be forgiving, helped me set my priorities straighter than they have ever been, and taught me how to listen.

"When you carry hate around for another human being you are not only hindering your soul, but you are also depriving yourself of the gifts that come out of friendship.

"A friend of mine became separated from her husband because he had had an affair with another woman. Then she dealt with a man who was terminal, a man who had also betrayed his wife, and who had spent the last half of his life looking for ways to make his wife forgive him. Listening to him, my friend was able to understand the sort of pain her husband was experiencing. She was able to forgive him and put their marriage back together. My own experiences haven't been as outward as this, but, yes, the dying can teach us much about how to live."

She sees all the tribulations of life, even the murder trial, as necessary, although hurtful ways to evolve and become a more authentic, a more caring, and a more candid person.

When the television movie on Anne's murder trial was aired, she didn't watch it. "I was working. And sure, some friends of mine taped it, so I could have watched it. But I have better things to do with my time. Now when people think of me and the murder trial they can attach all their images to Patti Duke," she laughs, "and not to me."

Nackey Loeb

The state of New Hampshire's motto—"Live Free or Die"—could have been written by Nackey Loeb. She is the publisher of New Hampshire's largest newspaper, *The Union Leader*, a position she assumed after her husband, William Loeb, who first ran the paper, died. Outspoken on the issue, Nackey believes strongly in freedom for the individual.

Gaining her own freedom has been a long battle for Nackey Loeb. In 1977, after a car accident left her paralyzed from the chest down, she had to learn the most elementary physical activities, like moving from a bed to a chair, all over again. Despite the severity of her injuries, she was ambitious and worked hard to rehabilitate herself so that she wouldn't have to be dependent on others for the rest of her life.

Today Nackey Loeb lives in a farmhouse in Goffstown, a small rural area outside of Manchester, New Hampshire. Several neighbors have wishing wells in their yards and everyone's mailbox is accompanied by another bright blue box where *The Union Leader* and *The Sunday News* are delivered.

It is May and the leaves have turned a vivid green. Birds are chirping, but snowmobiles are still parked in driveways and the "Frost Heaves" signs that are posted along the winding roads are proof that New England winters are long.

Her farm, Brindle Ledge, has a sign that is adorned with a reclining horse. It says "Boarding, Training, Sales, New England Custom Race Horses, Feeding, Hay, Grain and Shavings." Nackey Loeb's house sits on a hill behind a large barn where several teenagers are loading hay onto a truck. A large American flag waves on top of a tall pole and a stone statue of the American Eagle stands in front of her long, brown, shingled house.

Nackey is sitting in the foyer and with the wave of her hand, she gestures me for me to come in. Even though she's in a wheelchair, she seems athletic. Years of horse-back riding, tennis, skiing and salmon fishing have made her upper-body movements agile and natural. Her strong features seem to have been softened by age. She has a cap of beige-gray hair and wears no make-up. She's wearing a lavender-pink blouse and matching slacks that drape colorfully over her slender figure.

She escorts me into the living room. A large window looks out onto a field full of grazing horses. The room is filled with paintings, mostly landscapes. A small one, "The Donkey who Runs with the Dogs," was done by Nackey.

For Nackey Loeb, other people make her life worth living. "I would say that the greatest thing that made me survive and be here now is that I was needed. Also, I had a feeling when I started to recover and began to figure out what happened to me, that I actually should not have survived. Even the doctors had told me this. So I figured that there's a purpose for my surviving, darn if I know what it is, but I better stick around and find out. The accident happened at a time when I was needed and I continued to be needed more and more.

"Before the accident occurred, my husband had prostate cancer. They operated. 'All clean and okay. There should be no more problems,' they said. In five years there was a little problem here and a little problem there. 'We can use some chemotherapy,' they said. We knew the cancer was spreading and that there might be some real problems coming up. It became darn necessary that I keep myself together.

"I discovered that when you marry a man in the newspaper business, you marry the business too. Because the paper was vitally important to Bill [as he was less and less able to work], I gradually took over more responsibility. The paper was at a standstill then, not making much progress. It needed help and I helped Bill by helping the paper.

"During Bill's sickness he needed me and after he died, the paper needed me. So there was a continuation.

"In the survival process, looking back, I've discovered that this accident strengthened me. I've become much more of a person. I had lived a pretty good life. My family always took care of me. My husband took care of me. There were some ups and downs, but I never had to deal with hard survival issues: 'Are we [financially] up against it? Where are we going to live next week because we might lose the house?' I didn't really have to face the hard stuff and the kind of accident I had puts you [in a place] all by yourself. [Am I] going to make it or not?"

Nackey's accident occurred in 1977, near Christmas time. "Bill and I were driving back from dinner with a Baptist minister friend of ours. It was a damp night and the road was wet. We went over a rise and hit ice, black ice. In black ice you just sit there and float totally helplessly. We skidded off the side, turned over and landed upside down. Bill [who was driving] was shaken up, but he was alright. What happened to me was that when the car landed, the part of the roof that was over me flattened all the way down to the dashboard. I'm one of those people who is fortunate that I *wasn't* wearing a seatbelt. I slipped underneath the dashboard and got jammed in there. I broke my back, but my head might have been taken off [if I had been wearing a seatbelt]."

When she awoke days later, Nackey Loeb lay helpless in an intensive-care unit. She breathed only with the aid of a respirator and she was heavily medicated against the pain of the extensive injuries she had sustained. "I had those hallucinations people have when they have been [severely injured or are very sick and are on pain medication]. I was absolutely convinced that the nurses were carrying scissors because they were going to kill me. I also thought they were running a drug ring at the desk. I had it down to the details on all these people who I was sure were against me.

"I couldn't talk so I communicated with my family by writing: 'The nurses have *scissors*, which I underlined several times. They said to me, 'Don't worry, we'll be right outside the door watching the nurses.'" She laughs softly and her eyes dance, then she lifts her body up from the chair for a minute by stiffening her arms, because staying in one position for too long can cause skin sores.

"I think pain medication takes away reality. You are in a completely defenseless and foreign position and you know something horrible has happened, so you have these little nightmares."

At the time, Nackey did not understand what had happened to her and she felt totally confused and helpless. The chaos she was experiencing, especially during the period when she was under the influence of pain medication, was terrifying. The way she was used to existing in the world was shattered, because what she depended on—her body—no longer could function.

"After it was all over, I had to go around to the nurses and apologize. 'You wouldn't believe what I thought you were going to do to me, so I apologize for what I said.' They said not to worry, that it happened all the time and was a result of the medication and that they were used to it.

"I had an oxygen tube and a machine that pumped air into me; I forgot how to breathe on my own, so they had to teach me how to breathe again. They said you can go 'cold turkey' or you can do it over a period of time. I said 'cold turkey,' and it was horrible. After 24 hours of agony, I said, 'Give me the pump back.'

"Eventually, they told me that it looked like my back was broken and that I might be paralyzed. There was also a chance that I might not be, because there was a place on my foot where when they stroked, I could feel it. Since [the neurological deficit] wasn't complete, they said, 'we can't tell what's going to happen.'

"I don't know if it made that much of an impression on me. One thing is that I was curious as to how a person handles [a disastrous situation like this]. I knew other people had handled personal disaster, but I wondered how I could do that. Maybe that was my survival process."

On some level, Nackey may have felt that she was suffering more than she could tolerate and therefore may have tried to ward off the seriousness of her condition. Accepting her paralysis would mean making a total change in her self-concept, her social role, as well as her work and family roles, and she was incapable of comprehending all of these changes at one time.

At this particular stage in recovering from a trauma, it is not uncommon for people to alternate their overwhelming fears with an inability to process threatening information. Denial can ward off panic and allow one to be in safe territory. It can also help one pace oneself. Panic is an extreme form of anxiety, and as psychologist Rollo May explained in his book, *The Meaning of Anxiety*, anxiety is when you cannot orient yourself in your own existence or comprehend your world. Nackey coped in large part by focusing on her husband.

"I felt worse for Bill than for me. He was going bonkers. He was trying to be polite and nice, but you could see that he blamed himself [for the accident] and that he was mad, mad at the world. He questioned, 'Why should this happen to my wife? What has she done?' It was such a tough time for him that I had the job of bolstering him up.

For Nackey, showing her husband that she was strong "didn't come out in words. For example, when I was doing my rehab exercises, I'd say, 'Look, I am wiggling my tummy,' and even though I didn't give a darn about reading the mail, I'd say to Bill, 'I've got to read the mail and see what's going on,' in an effort to show him that I could handle it. By doing that, I found out that I really was able to handle things that I didn't think I could.

"I had the good fortune to go to an excellent rehab center. I went there from a hospital where they did everything for you. In the first 24 hours, I discovered everybody was brutal and nobody gave a darn. I was scared and I thought, 'I want to get out of here. This is horrible.' It took me a couple of weeks to realize that they were deliberately trying to get me so mad and frustrated that I'd do something to help myself.

"I was very tired at that point and one nurse said, 'You know, you only have two choices. You can either lie down and spend the rest of your life in bed, or you can do these lousy exercises and push yourself to make yourself improve.'

"There was this Spanish fellow who, when he got mad, got all the way mad. He had a very thick accent. I heard him yelling, 'Why must I do [the exercises]? I have 30 nieces and nephews, and they are going to do everything for me.' I always wanted to meet those 30 nieces and nephews who were going to be stuck with him when he got out." She laughs and her smile crinkles up her eyes.

"Another thing I remember is some woman saying to me, 'Don't look ahead and try to figure out how you can handle it. Look back and see where you've been.' That stuck with me. What she meant was that two weeks ago I couldn't brush my teeth without resting in between, two days ago I couldn't shift myself from one side of the bed to the other and I couldn't reach my feet to put on my stockings. Now I could. That type of thing.

"If you concentrate on how far you've come, by the time you have to do harder things, you are more physically able to do them and you are more mentally and emotionally able to face it. Things like panicking when moving from the chair to the bed without falling off. I worried and worried about that and now I don't even think about it unless I'm thinking about something else and get too close to the edge.

"When I was in the rehab center—and I think they've gotten rid of it now, which is fortunate—they believed that when a person is in a wheelchair, it has to be pounded into them that they will never walk again. I resented that, my family resented it and Bill was furious about it. He was convinced that if we tried hard enough, we'd get over it. In many ways it was harder on Bill than it was on me.

"There's a time when your body and mind are ready to say, 'I'll never walk again. So what?' I don't think you can rush it. That time [when you are ready to handle it] comes from building up, getting capable of doing a series of little things. It doesn't get you to the top of the mountain, but each little rock you climb, like moving from the chair to the bed, makes you better.

"Somewhere along the line I was accepting. Faith was very important. I knew I was never totally alone. I was in the hand of God, a stronger force, a support there. Without [faith] I don't know if I could have gotten through that long period when Bill was getting worse, that long wait when we knew the inevitable. I don't know if I would've had the strength if I hadn't climbed over all those little rocks I talked about.

"You have to face [your problems]. In the past, when I had a sticky problem I'd do artwork. Like the Band-aid approach, I'd cover up my problems, but [this] I had to face head on.

"In many ways I can look at [certain aspects of what happened to me] as a blessing—such as the personal strength that I obtained and the character building. I became much more of a person after the accident. I had a sureness of what I wanted to do, an ability to handle things that I don't know if I could have done before.

"After Bill died, I remember going into the paper and meeting with the people and saying, 'Where are we going from here?' I was able to do that. I had a lot of competence and self-assurance. I also learned the art of self-inspection. 'Why are you here? What can you do? What are your tools and how can you best use them?' I didn't have the ability to walk, but I had other tools.

"I used to be a very shy person. Before Bill died, when I used to attend the meetings at the paper, much of the time I sat in the corner doing needlework or something, absorbing all that was going on, but not asserting myself. Then suddenly, I was the publisher and I darn well had to assert myself. The paper was coasting, and it was terribly important to have everybody realize that the paper was still as strong, would still continue in its outspoken ways and that it would still be the state paper of New Hampshire. I was lucky. Bill left me a fine team of bright, dedicated people to work with. It was up to me to convince these people that it wasn't the end of the world when Bill died."

William Loeb had had a mammoth desk and when Nackey first assumed his position, she sat on the side of it. As she became more confident, she moved closer and closer toward the middle, until she felt comfortable sitting in the center. "Bill was always a person who had self-confidence that he could handle anything. I don't think I was ever like that. Eventually I thought, 'Well I guess I better handle it. Nobody else is around to do it.'"

When asked how she coped with Bill's death, she says, "It was such a slow process. It sounds inhuman, but I learned to face and accept that Bill was dying. He just gradually and slowly got worse and worse. He got to the point that he had to go back to the hospital and he was out of it more often than not. You'd go to visit him, and you didn't know whether or not he could hear. You talked to him, in case he heard you, in case he would know you were there. His dying was just one more little step.

"I'm not scared of dying. I don't know if that's because I got so close to the process during the accident. I don't remember going through a tube with a blinding light that you hear people talk about. I think dying is a natural process, and I'll hang in there as long as I can.

"I think there's a God who is playing an important part in deciding our fate. We are not captains of our ship, nor are we masters of our soul. There has to be a blind acceptance and we're not allowed to know the reason why things happen. For instance, it doesn't bother me that I don't know why I had the accident and why I was wedged under the dashboard. It happened, so I've accepted it. That acceptance carries me through."

Still, Nackey Loeb says that she is not a Pollyanna about the accident. There are still painful moments. "Little things trigger them. I have a golf cart set up so I can go buzzing around, down to the barn and through the fields whenever I feel like it. When I come back, the wheelchair is sitting there by itself. That always hits me, because it's the only time I ever see the wheelchair—that little prison I have to fit myself into—by itself. It's always beneath me. It's a funny sensation, a surprise. Like looking at myself from somebody else's point of view. It's like saying, 'Hey, that's you sitting there.'"

It is also painful when she has the urge to go outside with her grandchildren and play with them in the grass. When her husband was alive, their day began with two hours of tennis or, if they were in Nevada, horseback riding. Although Nackey no longer rides, horses are right outside her back window and she spends a lot of time watching them. "It's not a bad deal," she teases. "Other people do all the work [of caring for the farm]."

Nackey Loeb maintains a sense of vitality by knowing that she is part of forces larger than herself. She lives in a framework of connectedness to her children, her grand-children and nature. To her, these things make life worth living.

Richard Herrmann

"Dick kept telling me not to short-change myself," says
Violet Morin, a former student who, after having four
children, decided to go to college even though she was in
her late thirties. "He told me life is filled with surprises
and that I should go for my dreams. I never would have
gone to graduate school at Harvard if it weren't for him.
Dick changed my life." She's not the only one of his
students to feel this way. Dick Herrmann has dedicated
his life to encouraging and inspiring his students to grow,
and for most of them, the encouragement he offers is
imprinted forever on their lives.

Herrmann's office is at Norwich University in
Northfield, Vermont on the second floor of a three-story
wooden house with a large porch. Just across from his
doorway, the first thing I notice when entering is a large
photograph of two young boys, around three and six years
old, in swimsuits. Only the torso of the brown-haired,
younger boy is visible so that the older boy takes up most
of the picture. With a crown of wheat-colored hair, he
looks out unexpectantly with what a friend of
Herrmann's—the poet Colette—described as a seriousness which "...comes straight from behind the retina,
speaking the sort of terror children bear, not knowing it
might get easier, not knowing that they won't die of it."
The boy is Eddy, Dick's son, who did die in an automobile
accident in 1977.

Sitting amid the plants and books, Herrmann charts his journey through the pain he suffered when his son died. He also discusses the spiritual growth he acquired as he struggled against his feelings of anger and bitterness at his loss. He has soft brown hair, a handsome face and a dynamic personality; he is serene, yet at the same time, exhilarating. My awareness of being alive seems very sharpened in his presence.

In some ways, having a doctorate in human development from Harvard University helped Herrmann have a better understanding of the pain of his son's death and what he was going through, but it wasn't enough to actually provide any kind of serious help. He gradually realized that spiritual movement was essential. But how could he reconcile spiritual yearnings with his scientific and intellectual mindset? He wanted—somehow—to find a way to keep his son alive. This caused him a major struggle with rage and disillusionment.

He begins his story by telling me about the accident. "The boys and I were looking at cross country skis in St. Johnsbury when it started to snow. The snow was wet and heavy. We had a Volkswagen, and Willie, my youngest son, was in the back and Eddy was in the front. Eddy had asked for a comic book. He had just started to read a comic book that he loved. He was cuddled up in the front seat, oblivious to anything else but his book. He hated seat belts, so I didn't make him wear them. I slipped mine on instinctively, but I didn't make him do that because I didn't want him to holler. We'd had such a nice day." His soft voice trails off and his mind lingers.

"A few minutes later, [as we were] driving back, a car came around a curve too fast, skidded right into our lane and hit us head on. Eddy died that night." His mouth twitches in response to pain, but he takes a deep breath and continues. Dick, too, was hurt. "I was delirious for the most of two months [following Eddy's death]. I never even knew I was in St. Johnsbury Hospital, or Mary Hitchcock Hospital before that. I had head injuries, cuts, a shattered leg, and I spent the next four and a half months in 50 pounds of traction. Willie was all right, although he'd been thrown around quite a bit.

"My next image is of my wife Barbara standing beside my hospital bed. I said to her, 'I killed him' and she said, 'No, no, no.'

"My father, old and still quite mobile at 77, came all the way from New York, but I can't remember [the visit] because I was so delirious on morphine. My leg was smashed in several places, and because of the head injuries, the doctors couldn't operate. Two weeks later, they did operate and put my leg back together. When they took me off morphine, I regained consciousness."

As he talks, Dick takes off and puts on his glasses, and at critical moments and thoughts, he makes eye contact with me over the top of them. The head injuries have left Dick with vision problems; the bottom half of everything he sees looks double.

"How did I cope? I don't know. [Because I was in the hospital, which was] 100 miles from home, I could see Barbara and Willie only on weekends. They were wonderful. I was also very lucky to have three friends near Hamilton, Bill and George, colleagues with whom I had taught in Boston, and Susan, the sister of a present colleague. I was never isolated. They made sure I had a visit every day; it was extraordinary friendship. Colleagues from the college and friends visited and wrote. Our good friends, Ellen and Louise, wrote poems about Eddy's death which were later published. Willie's kindergarten class sent paintings for my hospital wall. The warmth from family and friends was incredible.

"But to go in the direction I need to go, to fill the void, to quench the rage, to deal with the question 'Why?' and to find meaning"—these are the questions Herrmann has trouble finding the answers to.

"My father was an Episcopalian. Evidently the hospital knew that, because the Episcopal chaplain, Karen, who was studying to become a priest, came to see me every day. She was vibrant, intelligent, sensitive and a pioneer in the ordination of women priests. She also was perceptive. Very smart. Although she couldn't have known that I had abandoned anything to do with the church a long time before, she somehow knew not to talk about religion right away.

"We talked about Eddy. She was wise, profound, funny. When I told Barbara about our fine talks, Barbara asked if she might meet Karen. 'Are you kidding?' I said. 'Of course!'

"Barbara herself had grown up in a non-religious family, but [because of] her conversations with Karen, Barbara converted to Christianity. I realized the church might be something I needed.

"Sitting there day after day after day, hour after hour after hour with 50 pounds hanging from my leg, I realized I needed to work hard to keep from becoming a bitter, despondent man. It had taken me a week just to sit up. I knew that could happen and I didn't want that; somehow I had to avoid it. Eventually, through my talks with Karen, I decided that it was Christianity which taught the lessons of love and forgiveness that were the lessons I needed to learn.

"But it wasn't easy. More of a problem than it might seem. As a kid I'd been sent to Sunday School, but what I call a college 'deconversion' came very easily and lasted." Still, when Barbara and I were married, we talked about our spiritual lives. We didn't want to neglect that. We decided to experiment. We attended several Friends Meetings and liked them and often the actuality of them. To me, it seemed the direction we would go."

Then there was a crisis that drove Dick away from religion yet again. "Our first baby died. The placenta had separated from the uterus. He was born ten days after he was due and died two days later. If he had lived, he would have been severely palsied, so we understand now that his death was probably a blessing. Destiny. But it didn't feel that way then. My most important goal was to have a family—have a wife, children and to be a father and husband—to establish a unit. For that to be curtailed so quickly was sad. So, we stopped attending Friends Meetings.

"But the following June I did go back. I attended a conference which included a Quaker Meeting. With some misgivings, I went, but it didn't work. I'm not the type of person who walks out of things he doesn't like. But as I sat there, I realized that if I said what the spirit moved me to, what was in my heart, [I would have voiced very angry feelings]. I would have stood up, clenched my fist, and said, 'If this is the kind of God you are, I don't want anything to do with you.' So, I left. That crystallized my disaffection with anything that had to do with religion."

Later, however, still constantly struggling with his grief over Eddy's death, Herrmann turned back to religion. "For me to come back to [religion] or to even consider coming back was an important move for me. At first, it was simply an intellectual decision. I knew that the lessons I wanted to learn, needed to learn, lay in Christianity. I did not want to be a bitter, angry man for the rest of my life. My first baby had died and now my second son had died, too." Herrmann pauses to describe Eddy. "He was brilliant and physically he was magnificent. He looked like his mother. He had her beauty. He was exciting, smart, fun and a leader. We had become close. Then for all of that to go, well...."

"I wanted to keep Eddy alive. I needed to keep him from death, if that's the way to put it. I could only see one way to do that; to keep Eddy from death, I needed to take my love for him back into the world. That was the only way to keep both him and me alive. I concluded that the best help I could get [to achieve this] was from a Christian message.

"But formal observance, attendance at church, was still beyond me. Barbara's conversation was the first real nudge. She kept saying, 'Why don't you try?' Then she found out the church choir needed a male bass for Christmas. I was still reluctant. But it was finally the music, something that I'd always loved, that tipped the scales.

"When I began attending church, it was a terrific intellectual and spiritual struggle to try to make sense of it for myself. I cried at every baptism. I had to struggle with many doubts. Here was a religion I'd had trouble with, but now the message of Jesus seemed crucial to me. I wanted to understand it, to pay attention to the lesson of love. The message of forgiveness. My task was to come to some kind of resolution, but it was hard.

"I am an academic who loves proof, even if it's rarely available, and that kind of thinking made me have many doubts. If there is a loving God, why is there so much pain? Why does God do this kind of stuff to people? Why is there so much anguish, famine, hurt in the world? My own pain seems virtually inconsequential in magnitude to what lies elsewhere. If you believe in a god, where does God's power stop? Did God kill Eddy and our baby, Freddie? Did God do that to teach me a lesson because I needed to learn something? Did God do this to me or was it an accident? Are there accidents in God's world? Is God ultimate order? Does God oversee everything, or are there elements of chaos still around? I had to find my way through some of these contradictions before I could make a full commitment. I made a conscious decision not to be embarrassed about trying." Herrmann realized that he wanted to find God if God would let him.

"About two years later friends asked us if we'd like 'to make a Cursillo,' which is a short course in Christianity, a movement that began in Spain, in Mallorca. Cursillo starts with a three-day meeting. Not a retreat. Eventually we went, each on separate weekends. It was powerful for each of us. Short talks are given by lay people on topics like community, action and study. A clergy member talks about grace, obstacles to grace—I wondered why one couldn't say 'sin'—and the sacraments. After each talk, we gathered at round tables in groups of about six for discussion.

It's serious and fun, there's joking and tears, wonderful singing and lots of hugging, even among men, and wonderful singing. It was spiritual for me in many ways, but perhaps most importantly in the way it affected my relationship with men. I have been lucky all my life in having good friends, good men friends and good women friends. But before this, I couldn't have imagined feeling love for others the way I did there and have ever since. I remember debating with myself whether this was just an unusually good encounter group. All that hugging. Sure, an accepting and trusting environment was created by sharing, sharing in ways that some had known before. But this had more substance than an encounter group. I'd seen encounter groups myself and I recognized the difference. Underlying the warmth, the joy and the tears was the continuity of Christian commitment to a solid message. I couldn't have conceived of anything like this before.

"It was a dramatic moment for me, personally and spiritually. It convinced me that my love for my son was part of God's love, Jesus's love, and it further convinced me that not only did I want to manifest that love in the world, but that I could.

"So I've been moving through the grief and trying to handle it by doing what I said I would do; by trying to take my love for Eddy back into the world. One result is more profound friendships than I've ever known before and as I said, I've had the good fortune to have good friends. Another is an active life in the church community. I'm on the governing board for Vermont Episcopal Cursillo. I participate on weekends. Connected with that movement and church, but also outside of that realm, I feel that my ability to carry my love for Eddy out into the world is growing and deepening.

"It seems now that my first task was to search for reasons why Eddy's death could possibly have happened, and even when I couldn't find any, then to refuse to let my love for my boy, my Eddy, get buried in rage. The question of whether his death somehow happened for a purpose still lurks within me. I don't really believe that it did, but let's climb into that frame of reference for a minute. If the accident happened, if Eddy and the baby died, if all this was done purposefully by a God who has decided to teach me something I needed to know, put it this way—what I needed to learn as a person that God might have shaken a finger at, yes, I can think of what it might be. There's been in me a kind of self-centeredness and egocentricity that I recognize. I was going to say I don't pay attention to that, but in fact I do. I've always wanted to be a fair, decent, sensitive person, and I've always wanted to be a generous person. I do think the self-centered part has changed. I don't think I'm completely different, but I think I'm a better person now.

"It's been hard on our marriage, too. Barbara's style of grieving was very different from mine, and we found it hard to support each other in our grief. At first it seemed Barbara needed to flee. She put 60,000 miles on the car driving the Vermont country roads. It was, she says, her way of meditating. I wanted to talk, to connect, and I felt pushed away. I wanted to share, not in the sense of her assuming any of my burden—her devastation was as deep as mine—but sharing something important that had happened to us both. And sharing love. I don't know when I finally understood that it was a different style of grieving and not a rejection. But I understand it now. It has taken a great deal of patience and tolerance on both our parts.

"Now the academic in me jumps in. We know how varied people's learning styles are. Similarly, if we might recognize and tolerate different styles of grieving, that might help. But I'm not sure, because feelings of grief and loss are so deep and sharp and difficult. Bringing rationality to such kinds of feelings may not be all that helpful a way of working with them. I guess mainly we need to try to listen and understand, and to be tolerant and fair, and to be patient. At one point while I was still in the hospital, Barbara's grief was so severe that she was afraid that she would harm herself, and she even thought she wanted to be hospitalized. By the time I got home [from the hospital], her depression was less severe, but by then I didn't have much to offer her, and she didn't have much to offer me. It was a constant struggle. One that required constant and conscious effort.

"How has the accident changed my philosophy of life? It's hard to say for sure. I've always been aware of the preciousness of every moment and of the illusions of objectives. Yes, of course, we all have to have goals. I help my students and my son Willie set goals. But it's important that we not let the goal blot out the magic of any particular moment, that we don't run away from the preciousness of the moment. Often that can be paradoxical, because not every fine moment is a surprise, but it's sometimes in those momentary joys that the richness of being alive comes through the most, rather than through long-term goals. Moments I had with Eddy are precious to me. Almost every moment can have a preciousness that I want to be aware of as much as I can.

"I'm not sure how much this insight has to do with the accident or my age. I'm old enough now that many of my life tasks have been completed. Oh, there may be some career advances ahead, and I wouldn't mind earning more money than I do, but there's a piece of me that doesn't give a crap about what is going to happen next. I did receive tenure, and I cared about that, of course, but it was not genuinely rewarding. It was practical; my professional path could have been bumpier without it.

"I'm told I'm ultra purposeful, but there's a piece of me that believes that nothing really matters. That there isn't any meaning anywhere. And that the only meaning is in what gives one pleasure. The rest I don't know. No, I do know more than that. I know that there are many pleasures. Yes, sensory and sensual ones, aesthetic ones, emotional ones, spiritual ones. I also know that many of those pleasures are more available if one is systematic about going after them. Even though there's a piece of me that thinks things are absurd, I believe my task is making sense out of things the best way I can. I am more comfortable with myself making sense out of things than in thinking there's no reason for living. And the lessons of love and forgiveness I learn continually from Christianity help me do that.

"The pain, the hurt of Eddy's death is constantly there. It never goes away. You don't get over it, even if you do eventually find ways past it and find new joys and satisfactions. Although it's hardest around anniversaries, holidays and his Thanksgiving birthday, I always wish he was here. He was just splendid. Breath-taking, quick and decisive. He was all the wonderful things that Barbara is. Willie is more like me, more of an intellectual, maybe slower and more thoughtful than Eddy. Eddy wanted to do things, to get things done. He was courageous and fun. When he was six he wanted to jump off the roof of the vacation cabin we have. I was shoveling snow off the roof. He wanted to come up there, too. Then he wanted to jump off. So I climbed back down, made sure there was a big pile of snow with no branches or rocks in it, made sure it was soft, and he jumped. Off a 15-foot roof! At age six. He loved it, and I loved his courage and daring."

Another way Dick Herrmann deals with his feelings when he misses his son is to write to him. A graduate school friend suggested this and his letters keep his son's memory alive. In one letter, he writes, "One particular memory flashes brilliantly to mind: you at Good Harbor Beach in Gloucester. We'd walk through the dunes to the edge of the beach. Immediately from there you'd fly off to the edge of the ocean, where you'd almost never stop running at all, your swift little legs churning and spinning under you constantly. That image of you is etched sharply and vividly in my mind."

Although writing helps Dick feel connected to his son, and religion helps him deal with his anger and find new satisfactions, he still feels the injustice of his son's death. "Now I feel robbed of the chance to be with him, and now that Willie has reached adolescence and is testing limits, I wonder what Eddy would have been like. He would have been something. I really didn't want more than two children, but out of three, I have one left, and that leaves me feeling cheated. I'm angry about that, and that's why it was important for me to find some positive ways through the morass. Yes, the anger really could eat me up.

"But now we come to another paradox, because at the same time, I'm also very conscious of how lucky I am, and how marvelous my life has been. I have a talented, handsome wife. A splendid, gifted son—athletic, musical, artistic, mature. So I do have the family I always wanted. I've had jobs I've loved, and a fine Vermont life. I've lived in enough other places to know the difference, and I feel very fortunate. There's much of me that is satisfied.

"I'm especially grateful for my work. I reach out to students. I find it thrilling when they do good work. I like them. They may recognize that I bring something personal to the task and that I care about them. I've had some counseling training, for example, so that kind of communication is not alien to me. But it's a purposeful awareness now. It's another chance to help, to serve. Even though I'm seen by most of my students as relatively demanding, most end up liking me a lot. I'm grateful for that.

"My life has been enriched since Eddy's death and, through the accident, I have learned to love in ways that I could never have known before."

Rabbi Harold Kushner

Usually we are confident in our ability to control things,"
explains Rabbi Harold Kushner, "but then suddenly we
learn that the things that matter most in our lives we
cannot control." At such times, at the limits of our own
strength, we turn to God. "There are no atheists in
foxholes," he says, "because such times bring us face to
face with our limitations."

Kushner had to face his own limitations when he
learned that his young son had a terminal disease.
"Aaron was three when the seriousness of his illness was
first diagnosed, when it got a name and we were told it
would shorten his life drastically and he would die in his
early teens. He died 11 years later almost to the day."

Kushner's voice seems matter-of-fact about his son's
death. He has talked about it so many times—on TV talk
shows, in sermons, with bereaved families, and in three
bestselling books—but there's still a sadness in his eyes
and a downward turn of his mouth.

Big-boned and with gray hair under his yomulke, he
sits in the embrace of his high-backed desk chair with
his arms crossed in front of his chest. We are in his office
at Temple Israel in Natick, Massachusetts. Numerous
certificates and diplomas—several of them printed in
Hebrew—adorn the walls. Above his desk is a large
silkscreen of a woman in reds and blues. The rest of the
wall is covered with full bookshelves.

101

Included among the collection are two volumes of his latest bestselling book, *Who Needs God*. Although he has published four books, the second one, *When Bad Things Happen to Good People*, on the bestseller list for an entire year, is how most people know him. The book describes the crisis of faith he experienced after learning that his son had progeria, a rapid, premature aging disease, and that his boy would never grow more than three feet tall, eventually looking like a little old man in a child's body. "Coming to terms with having a child with an incurable condition had to be done right away," Rabbi Kushner says. "Could I continue as a religious man? I had counted on the world working in a certain way and it was not working that way. I was angry with God, disappointed, hurt and felt cheated. What could I have possibly done that we could be punished like this? I'm not perfect, but I thought there's no way my family deserves this if there's any justice in the world.

"Could I continue as a rabbi where a large part of my work is either officiating in services where we celebrate other people's children growing up or counseling people to go on trusting the world. If I could no longer affirm those two things with any sense of integrity, could I continue to serve in this capacity?" His large hand gestures at the diplomas and certificates on the wall and his voice and eyes have some of the tension in them that he felt then—when he was torn between the comfort of the ideas he had grown to trust and live by and the uncomfortable need to change them.

"I didn't want to be angry with God. My faith in God was very important to me. This isn't simply what I do for a living. This is who I am. So I worked for some way to maintain my faith in the goodness of God without saying that my son Aaron deserved it or that my wife and I deserved it or that in some way God was justified because sometime down the road we'd be better off because of it.

"This was in 1966 when people were not all that amenable to therapy for that kind of situation. Several years later my wife and I did go for therapy to deal with the fact that Aaron was dying. At the time we couldn't tell Aaron, who was only three years old, about his condition and we were reluctant to tell our family. So, we had to deal with it ourselves, privately.

"I read everything I could—prose, poetry, philosophy, fiction and nonfiction—on the question of children dying and their parents coping with it. I obsessed on [the dilemma] because I couldn't talk to anybody about it. I had a book in my library called *Dimensions of Job*. At the end of the book, I read this essay by Archibald MacLeish in which I found the key to the whole problem. MacLeish doesn't quite say it the way I do, but the way he phrased it helped me to come to the conclusion I came to.

"God doesn't control everything in the world. This is an unfair world and God's role is to help us survive in an unfair world so that we know that we're not trying to do it alone. As soon as I read that, I was cutting the Gordian knot; everything fell into place. This was the winter of 1967. For the next ten years I used this [idea] when counseling bereaved families and in sermons to help people cope with the tragedies in their lives."

In Kushner's new understanding of the universe, God created the magnificent order that supports life, but He does not give crashing airplanes, multiplying cancer cells or a child's rapid aging disease instructions. There are pockets of disorder in the universe, but if we turn to Him during times of suffering, He will provide a sustaining presence in the bedrock beneath our fear. He will help us accept the chaos in the universe.

On August 1, 1967 there was a tragedy in Kushner's congregation; a four-year-old boy was killed by a school bus. Rabbi Kushner was asked to comfort the family. "I strongly identified with them because of their loss. I was able to try on them the same resolution I had found for myself. When I saw how comforting they found it, I knew I was on the right track.

"The resolution was this: if I had to choose between a powerful God who is not good or a good God who is not all-powerful, I think the more religious answer would be to affirm God's goodness as opposed to His power. Since then, I have read a passage by Carl Jung which says we find it comforting to believe in an all-powerful God, but God doesn't have to be all-powerful just because it makes us more comfortable. I think one of the major purposes of religion is to assure us that the world is a reasonable place—not necessarily fair, but reasonable."

Kushner is reminded of the powerful laws of nature when he watches a storm pelting the earth with rain and illuminating the sky with flashes of lightning. He is comforted by a sense that there is a great and powerful God, but he doesn't believe that God would prevent the lightning from striking him if he went out in the storm. Nor does he feel that God could have prevented his son's illness just because Kushner lived a compassionate and religious life.

"Most people assume they suffer because of their sinfulness or because they might benefit from the tragedy somewhere down the road, but it didn't work for me to think that an innocent child would suffer because of some benefit down the road."

The Kushners didn't tell Aaron, the rest of their family or Aaron's teachers about the diagnosis. "Aaron was small and we just said [to others] that he wasn't growing as fast as other kids. As he grew older and the disparity grew more marked, we told people, 'We don't know. The doctors are trying to figure it out.' Partly, it wasn't a big issue because we had him in a small school where everybody knew him. At first meeting he looked strange, but once you got to know him, you didn't notice it that much. He didn't let his physical problems distort his personality. We thought he was beautiful."

The Kushners didn't focus on the possibility of Aaron's death; they had other concerns such as coping with the day-to-day limitations of a child who had physical problems and helping their son deal regularly with other people's dubious reaction to the way he looked. Kushner says, "You know how teenagers who are 13 and 14 are all wrapped up in their body image? Here was a child who was seriously deformed yet so at peace with himself that his classmates would come to him and talk to him about their problems. He was the sort of kid other kids enjoyed. Aaron was very bright. He was a little kid but he had a playful intelligence.

"We always worked on the assumption that he would live. We thought about the future even when he was six months away from dying. We talked about a high school placement for him." The Kushners began to wonder if they should insist that Aaron be treated like a normal child when he was not a normal child, and together Kushner and his wife entered therapy to sort through their feelings.

"There was a lot of denial on our part. Therapy helped us get past the denial and helped us anticipate the end and not be blown away by the grief when it came.... Therapy helped us grieve."

In the last year of his life, Aaron's health started to go downhill. In June 1977, the doctors discovered that Aaron had developed congestive heart failure which is part of the terminal phase of progeria. "Aaron had to catch his breath when he walked," Kushner explains. "Toward the end, he had to sleep standing up because his lungs would fill up with fluid if he lay on his back.

"My wife sat with him and told him his condition was fatal and that he only had a few months to live. We asked him what he wanted to do while he was still physically able to do it. We talked about his funeral."

At first Aaron just cried, but then, because time was running out, he thought of three ways to have an interesting summer. He said he wanted to visit the Baseball Hall of Fame, to see an R-rated movie and to meet another kid with progeria. "He did the first two but not the third. Since then, we've met other kids with progeria, but at the time hardly anyone had even heard of the disease because of its rarity. Since my book came out ten years ago, Phil Donahue has done three programs on progeria and it is written about in the literature, but in Aaron's lifetime there was never anything mentioned about it. I don't think there are 20 kids alive today who have progeria.

"One of the reasons I wrote the book *When Bad Things Happen to Good People* was that Aaron, like a lot of children who realize they are dying young, was afraid he would be forgotten because his life was so short. We had to assure him that we would remember him. He wanted his story told and I said I would do my best to see that it got told.

"I wasn't prepared for his life to end so soon. I thought we'd have another year or two with him. It was ending too fast and he was slipping away. He was very sick when he died. He was bedridden and could barely talk and was in a lot of pain. So the terrible sense of loss we felt when he died was mixed with the feeling that at least his suffering was over."

Kushner waited a year and a half before he started to write his book. "If I had started right after his death, all I would have been able to articulate was my pain and loss. Since my book came out, I've heard from a lot of people who also have lost their children, many of whom also wrote books about [the experience] and fantasized that theirs would be an international bestseller like mine was. Generally, they made the mistake of beginning to write too soon, so [their books are] a chronology of the illness, the death, the bereavement and their emergence. Many of the books are mainly about how much they hurt. They talked about the first Christmas and going to the beach house for the first time after the death. The average person reads that kind of thing and says. 'It's really sad, but I'm not getting anything out of it.'"

Kushner had spent 11 years using his insights to comfort people and was able to place Aaron's death in a frame of reference that permitted him to affirm the religious values of his life. He chose his attitude toward his losses; "I had no control over whether Aaron would be sick or healthy. I only had control over how I would respond to it—whether to be embittered and jealous or more empathetic and sensitive.

"If my book helps people it is not just because of the ideas it contains but because of my personal witness. The theology without the personal dimension would not have nearly the same impact.

"Maybe it was easier for me to cope because I was better able to comfort others. But I never got to the point that I could affirm what was happening to us or say it was good and valid because it turned me into someone who could help others. The most I could do was to say it was unfair and tragic but that I might be able to get some good out of it. To say that what is tragic can actually be good creates a great deal of emotional dishonesty.

"One of the worst parts of being a victim of this kind of tragedy is your sense of helplessness. You wish you could take years off your life and add them to your child's. One of the ways of digging out of the sense of helplessness is to realize you are uniquely qualified to strengthen others. That's why the experience of publishing the book and going around the country speaking has been very therapeutic for me."

Unexpectedly having the book become a bestseller has changed Kushner's life in many ways. "I have a sense of validation that my ideas make sense. I moved to addressing a national audience rather than a local congregation, which gave me a different sense of who I am. How? I am a person who can help others heal wounds. I can go to any city in the country and lecture, and people I don't know come up to me and say I've changed their lives. That's an incredible experience. It happens all the time and I never get used to it. It's always something special.

"I was in Detroit recently and a woman came up to me. Her husband had been killed in an auto accident six months before and she said she never could have gotten through it if it weren't for my book. It's an indescribable experience. Here's this woman whose existence I didn't even know about and yet because of what I had been through, I was able to be a major influence on her life. I'm not helpless. I'm able to do something very important." Still, such experiences don't make Aaron's death a good thing." If I had to choose I'd rather be an average rabbi with a 28-year-old son. But I don't have a choice, so I do the best I can with the reality of the hand that's been dealt me.

"Just the fact that I continue to identify myself as a religious person is a choice I make that affirms the goodness of life. When people ask survivors of the Holocaust how they can still believe in God, they say they don't want to give the Nazis the satisfaction of stopping them from believing in the goodness of the world. 'I don't want to let them win.' The death of a child is tragic because life is precious. If tragedy robs us of our sense of the preciousness of life—if it seduces us to say it's all a crock and life isn't worthwhile and we shouldn't leave ourselves vulnerable—then we rob life of meaning.

"You can limit the power of the tragedy. This is from Viktor Frankl's *Man's Search for Meaning*. The one thing evil can't do is take away our choice about how we feel about it. If you choose to give up because of what you've gone through, then you become a witness for evil because you make it so strong.

"Had I given up and become a nonreligious person, then I would no longer be me. Religion is an important aspect of me.

"If you are a religiously committed person and you have learned what it means to open yourself to God, all you have to do in a specific situation is to say, 'I'm trying to do something hard. I don't think I can do it alone. I think I can do it if you are with me.' If you've spent your life with regular doses of personal and congregational prayer, you are comfortable opening up yourself to God like that and asking Him to replenish and strengthen you. If you are doing it for the first time, it's like trying to play tennis for the first time. It's terribly awkward.

"I don't think the problem is that people don't encounter God. The problem is that they don't recognize Him when they do encounter Him, when He is present in their lives." Kushner believes that God is present when people are tender, helpful and generous to each other. The fact that we feel so good when we go out of our way to do somebody a favor, that's an encounter with God. The sense of overwhelming relief we feel when we know we've done something wrong and find that people are capable of forgiving us, that's an encounter with God. And, to know we are capable of getting over being hurt and forgiving other people. It's hard to get through the day without encountering God four or five times.

"My question is not 'Who is God?' but 'When is God?' Ultimately, I believe in God because I always see ordinary people do extraordinary things. This, not any philosophical syllogism, is the proof that God exists. The most average people are capable of so much love and courage and resilience. They come up with qualities they did not know they had. Unless there really is a God, I can't imagine where they get these qualities."

Patricia Dean

Like medieval alchemists, psychologist Patricia Dean helps suicidal teenagers convert images of loss and despair into inner strength and hope. Dean's clients have been hospitalized after trying to hang themselves, or slitting their wrists or overdosing on medication. She helps them explore inner resources with artwork and storytelling. There they find healing symbols and transform helplessness into control, collapse into mastery and chaos into grace.

"When teenagers get into a crisis, they sometimes hold onto the negative and don't see that life has many ups and downs," Dean explains. "During the down moments, you find the answers. I use a metaphor from Joseph Campbell's work. We are all on a hero's journey, and who we are emerges from our story, which also brings up healing images." Dean has her clients draw their healing symbols onto a shield, similar to those used by knights in the Middle Ages. Their shields tell their stories and help them put their conflicts into words.

Dean's work with adolescents who have lost hope comes out of her own struggle to find it while her husband Rusty was dying of a fatal nerve disease. "Rusty went back and forth from life to death, staying in contact with me the whole time. He couldn't speak because of paralysis, but he went back and forth from this world to the next and you could see the ecstasy on his face."

In an airy sky-lit room of Dean's home, her blue eyes sparkle from a delicate face framed by a soft black pageboy haircut. In a blue dress, she sits on a blue wicker couch on a blue and pink rug into which butterflies, birds and flowers have been woven. Such images seem to bring inside the hum and buzz of nature outside the floor-to-ceiling windows which look out to a yard enclosed by a white picket fence.

Rusty's death was 15 years ago and Patti Dean has remarried. Her husband is an artist who made the sculpted table between us. Alligators are carved into the rich wood. A similar piece of his is in the Louvre Museum. Window sills are adorned with his unusual toys—a woman with a bird perched on her shoulder, a rocking horse, a stuffed witch with swan feet.

Dean gazes out the window as if into the past and begins to describe the journey that has brought her to the serene space she now inhabits. "Rusty and I were married for about 11 months. Our daughter had just been born and it was a real happy time for us. We were enjoying the thought of travel. Rusty was an officer in the Navy. He started to complain that he was getting out of shape. When he went running, it was like he was moving in slow motion. He began losing his balance and at times he even fell down.

"The Navy began a series of tests. They brought in a neurologist from Massachusetts General, but nobody knew what was wrong with him. His symptoms kept getting worse. First, he used a cane, then braces, then a wheelchair. It was scary. I was afraid the paralysis would creep up his body and he'd be in an iron lung. It was overwhelming. You had to hold on tight and be brave or you could fall apart." Dean speaks softly, but her voice has an undercurrent of urgency. "We were angry that they weren't doing anything quick enough to find the diagnosis. We felt helpless. There was evidence that the paralysis was spreading into his hands. With every little loss of strength, we'd sink a little more.

"His parents lived in England then, and we went over there and spoke to top neurologists. We also went to the Mayo Clinic here. All the doctors said, 'We don't know what it is.' Finally they diagnosed [Rusty's illness] as chronic idiopathic peripheral neuropathy. I began doing research and soon learned that it was a terminal disease. The doctors hadn't told us this.

"At one hospital where he went for tests, Rusty said, 'There's a guy down the hall who has what I have, but he's in a later stage. He's a vegetable.' We thought, 'Oh my God, this could happen to us.'" Her eyes grow wide as she remembers the shock and fear.

"We decided that we had to live for and celebrate every day. For everything we had to let go of, we felt something would come in to take its place. That's how we lived through those years.

"The Navy retired him. That meant [they knew that] the muscle and nerve damage wasn't going to stop, or if it did, too much damage had already been done. That was very hard. We had to let go. We couldn't dwell on it. We had to go on to the next step. Rusty enrolled in law school at Notre Dame where he had studied as an undergraduate. That was exciting, and we were able to feel hopeful again.

"We arrived there when our daughter Alison was about two. Rusty was in a wheelchair and since he was losing the use of his hands, he used a steno machine like they use in courtrooms. He spoke into a tape recorder. The first term he made all A's and one C. For one of the exams a secretary had transcribed his answers and there were so many spelling and grammatical mistakes that any professor would have given a C. Although he was very tired, Rusty made law review—a distinct honor.

"There was part of me that was very strong and another part that was emotionally drained. I had to bathe and dress Rusty and to do the same with Alison. It was tedious, so we had to find some lightness and humor.

Rusty was playful and wise. We never felt helpless. We'd say, 'This is shit.' But we didn't dwell on it. Somehow we felt everything was going to be okay. We bought a van and went camping. We built a house. We needed one with wheelchair ramps. There was a thread of joy in every day. When some goal we were striving for wasn't going to be there, we felt sad. Then we'd reevaluate and set different goals.

"We talked about his dying during the last two years of his life. I told him I didn't know what I'd do without him. My life was totally wrapped up in caring for him. The three of us were a closely knit unit. His family was in Europe and mine was unavailable and many of our friends were ready to graduate from law school. Rusty had to drop out the last year because he was too weak. It was a disappointment that he wasn't going to finish law school, but more important, it was another step closer to him dying.

"Before Rusty died he made tapes for Alison to play when she was older. He told her to celebrate every day. He spent the last year in bed. He was losing his sight and his mouth and tongue were paralyzed. He had to have a tube inserted into his stomach because he could no longer swallow.

"When his lungs filled with blood, he said, 'I can't go on. I'm leaving you.' At first I said, 'No, no, no,' but I wanted to help him die peacefully. Finally I said, 'It's okay.' He began to see himself on the other side and he seemed peaceful. 'Pretend I'm okay,' he said and he experienced himself as whole." Dean is silent as she lets this memory unfurl inside her like a magic scroll.

"When he finally died, I felt that he was soaring free and happy. People wondered why I was smiling. Bringing me through that process was a gift that gave me strength, hope and joy. I saw butterflies and would think of him soaring free of that shell that was his body. Everything opened up for me and suddenly there was this feeling of hopefulness and something within me came more alive. I knew I was on a journey and I could let him go. It freed me up to go on with my life. He gave me a joy, a gift which has always been with me ever since. People take life for granted. They aren't open to all the advantages they have. Rusty used to look at Alison and say, 'If only I could touch her cheek.'

"I had been raised in Catholicism, which looks outside to priests, to nuns and to God to save you. That wasn't working for me after Rusty's death. I needed to go inside and learn more about myself, so I turned to Eastern religion. I studied Jungian psychology. I had to face the pain and fear. If you repress the darkness, you won't be able to face anything. The darkness can turn to light.

"It was something I had to do. Something was pushing me along. I didn't have any choice in the matter. A lot of people came into my life and it seemed synchronistic. I went to this bookstore to buy a book on how to explain death to a one-year-old and this woman said, 'I think you would enjoy this class on death and dying I'm in and the class would benefit from your experience as well.' This happened one week after Rusty's death and I was changed by the class.

"I studied art therapy and movement therapy and I also began to work with people who were terminally ill. Because of the experience with my husband, I felt I had something to give, but I also knew that I had to try to get mastery over my grief. People had told Rusty and me that we were doing a good job, but Elisabeth Kübler-Ross was just beginning to write about death so [because most people didn't know much about how to cope with death] we didn't get much support. When Rusty died I used what I had learned was helpful to others, but also to heal my grief.

"When I was in college I was in a car accident. That was another pivotal event in my life, one that changed my direction. I was thrown 40 feet in the air. I remember being up in the air and seeing the car rolling. I'm not sure if this was an out-of-body experience or not. I came to when I hit the ground. I only had a broken pelvis, but could have broken my neck. I was saved and I felt there was some reason I was on earth. I was scared, but felt close to God. I didn't know what was ahead, but I knew my life was changing. I had been studying Spanish and I switched my major to special education."

In every crisis Patti Dean looks for meaning. "There are events I try to follow rather than trying to control. It's going with the flow and finding out what I'm being asked and trying not to fight it."

Through the Jungian therapist she was seeing, Patti met her second husband. "Peter was also interested in dreams and spirituality. He's an artist and was also exploring his inner experience. Getting married was the farthest thing from my mind at the time, but I felt bad that Alison didn't have a father. It was divine intervention. We were married after I had been a widow for two years.

"Then my dad committed suicide. I really fell to pieces. I had been emotionally apart from my father for many years and felt sad and guilty that I hadn't been able to help him and hadn't been with him through his suffering. I felt I could feel his pain. I had been with Rusty during his illness and he had had a happy death, while my father's death was a tragedy, a shock. I did a lot of art therapy on myself. I was physically sick and reached the bottom. I think it was an accumulation of all those years. I had acupuncture and massage therapy as a way to heal myself and to get stronger. Maybe I fell apart then because I was married to Peter and was able to fall apart.

"When I got better, I worked in a hospice. It was a way of mastering the grief process and reaching out to other people. I helped other people who were caring for someone with terminal illness. Just by sitting with me, young widows said they knew they could get through their grief and survive.

"I was trying to find an opening to look at a bigger picture. I felt I was given a message that said, 'There's more than what's here. There's something beyond, something greater than you are.' It's something I'd known but it's different to feel and experience it in your body.

"There's a piece of that higher source within us. We have to tap into it. I use dreams, meditation and guided imagery. Synchronicity is very important to me and so is the feeling that some force other than myself guides me.

"I was raised very differently. 'You are a shameful and guilty person and you need God's forgiveness or you will end up in purgatory.' Somehow this journey has enabled me to let go of that.

"I used to think that wisdom was on the outside, that other people knew the answers, that other people were going to tell me what to do. The priests and nuns knew what was best somehow. Rusty's death brought me close to my own resources and my own reasons. We have our own inner wisdom inside of ourselves. It has to be awakened and listened to. Along with that comes responsibility and becoming fully who you are. That's what 'spiritual' means to me: following your path and becoming who you are to the fullest.

"I use the image given to me by a friend, Rita, who is writing a book on guilt. We come into the world like the sun, full of joy. On a cloudy day the sun doesn't shine, but the clouds are really a distortion. They are messages that we are not getting along with our parents, our family or ourselves. They block who we are. We need to push through the clouds so our true nature can come forth."

Dean's true nature was revealed when she was vulnerable. "The defenses came down and I was more than what I thought I was." When Dean decided to become a clinical psychologist she wasn't sure she could get through statistics and writing a dissertation. But she'd learned that she had more resources and potential than she thought and so she decided to just push through the fear. She eventually wrote her dissertation from a voice in her own experience. When her study was presented to the faculty, she received a standing ovation.

When working with suicidal teenagers Dean uses everything she's learned from her own experience. One potent tool is her father's story. As a teenager her father had been a talented athlete, but he attended a small

Catholic school which lacked the facilities for him to excel. The coach of the local high school football team told him that if he transferred, he could be quarterback of the football team. He transferred, but the following Sunday a priest threatened from the pulpit to excommunicate his entire family. Dean's father capitulated and his dreams dashed, he returned to Catholic school. "This became the story of his life, one that he was never able to transform," Dean says. His rite of passage was denied him. This unfulfilled moment festered, and obvious or not, it became the personal myth that informed his life. It was like a ghost in the room.... Three months after he retired from a lifelong job that he disliked, he committed suicide."

No one saw her father's strength, Dean says, and no one helped him tap it. "No one really listened to his heart's desire, what his hopes were, what his dreams were, what his conflict was. No one spent the time to really sit and listen to those images, stories and emotions." This, Dean says, is the way teenagers get lost.

Learning from her father's experience, Dean designed an exercise that is something like a ritual to help adolescents through their transition into adulthood. "I used a Jungian paradigm which was close to my heart and my own healing. I believe there's power in the unconscious. There's potential there, if you listen to your dreams and fantasies and can tap into them."

She illustrates: "Joanne, one of the girls in my research study, had a happy memory of sitting on a sofa, watching soap operas, smelling Italian food cooking and knitting afghans with her grandmother, who had recently died. Joanne had been sexually abused and the main issue in her treatment had been the abuse, but nobody was dealing with the loss of the grandmother." Dean had Joanne bring the afghan to the hospital and symbolically draw on the strength of her grandmother to deal with the sexual abuse. Reviving the connection to her grandmother gave Joanne a base from which to build other trusting relationships.

Later, with her mother, Joanne brought the afghan

to her grandmother's grave. They spread the afghan out, sat on it and recalled happy moments shared with her grandmother. Joanne and her mother cried together and, in addition to other benefits, the connection between mother and daughter was strengthened.

Another client who worked with Dean was Jamie, a 14-year-old who tried to hang himself. Before he died, he was found unconscious by his adoptive father, who immediately performed mouth-to-mouth resuscitation. Jamie had asked his adoptive parents for a gun, and later a sword, but given his recent suicide attempt, of course they wouldn't give him such things. Dean began her work with Jamie and guided him through exercises designed to evoke symbols. The first was a slit wrist, which he said represented having been given away by his birth mother. When asked to find a vision for the future, Jamie drew a paintbrush, to suggest his dream of becoming an artist. When asked for an image of something that could help him on his journey, he drew a pen. While integrating all these images into a shield, Jamie realized he could write about things that bothered him and the people that made him mad. Jamie asked his parents for a Mont Blanc pen, which he discovered was mightier than a gun or a sword.

While Dean has her ups and downs, she believes that in life one must venture out into the world as well as going inward and replenishing the self. After the exhausting outward stretch of a doctoral program and fellowships, Dean feels that she is entering a new transitional phase of her journey which will be more inward and nurturing of her inner processes.

Dean remembers her own halting steps toward transformation. "I tried not to be afraid of looking at those parts of myself I didn't like. It took courage but I had no choice." It is that same progression that she offers the teenagers in her care. She helps them clear away the clouds so that the joy of their futures can shine through.

Donna Jenkins

At the Dana Farber Cancer Institute in Boston, psychologist Donna Jenkins brings a touch of joy and magic into a world of sadness and terror. To help the children with cancer leave their pain behind, Jenkins offers them a fantasy life that includes magic carpet rides, kings and clowns and trips to see Santa Claus. She helps them enter a special world of stories of knights on horseback who slay dragons. They can leave their sterile hospital beds and enter a palace where they are the heroes who defeat the enemies. When children are able to enter magical worlds, they are sometimes able to obtain a sense of control over their illnesses.

The clinic at the hospital provides the props: a completely furnished three-foot-tall doll house, dress-up clothes, a huge assortment of puppets, numerous jars of Playdough and crayons, and paints and paper.

Chemotherapy treatments often make people bald and Jenkins uses humor to help them accept their shiny, hairless scalps. "I'm working with this six-year-old girl with leukemia who's in her second remission. Her grandmother makes her these beautiful head bands to match her dresses, but she chooses to paste these Harley Davidson biker decals on her bald head and we have fun giggling about that. She laughs when I tell her that it only takes her two seconds to take a shower because she doesn't have to wash her hair."

This little girl doesn't know that Jenkins herself once used humor on herself to accept her own partial baldness. At 15, when she had cancer, Donna and one of her friends drew faces on the bald part of her scalp. Then, to scare one of Jenkins' sisters who was squeamish about the hairless part of Donna's head, as a joke they showed the faces they had drawn.

"Not one of my patients knows that I too had cancer because they need to concentrate on themselves," Jenkins says. "In indirect ways, I use my experience to validate their experience. One girl I worked with said, 'They just view me as a disease. It's like cancer is tattooed on my forehead.' I really responded to that because when I was sick, I also wanted other people to view me as normal. The person was there before the sickness and, God willing, the person will be there afterwards."

Jenkins discovered this idea of using imagination through one of her patients. "There is this seven-year-old girl with leukemia who had to stay in the sterile room because she was having bone marrow transplants. She had developed a bad rash on her backside from the treatments. It was Halloween and she had this wonderful princess outfit with a crown but she wasn't allowed to wear underwear because it would have interfered with the healing of the rash. Not wearing underwear didn't fit her fantasy, so she refused to wear the costume. She cried and was inconsolable. I tried reasoning with her, I tried anticipating her concerns, I tried everything but nothing worked.

"Then I tried to connect with her sense of what every other seven-year-old in America was able to do that she couldn't. I had memories of myself in gym class, not having the strength to do what all the other kids could do. Then I said to her, 'Have you ever heard of magic underwear? I should tell you about magic underwear. You can wear them all the time, even with bandages and medicines. They come in all colors, shapes and designs.'

"I held the imaginary bag open and rooted through it until I found a pink and purple pair which I tried on.

They were too small and got caught around my knees. That got a giggle out of her. I held the imaginary bag out for her and she went through it. She found a pink and purple pair with kittens on them. Her grandma and I raved as she tried them on, giggling. She was able to wear her princess outfit after that.

"I think using whimsy and fantasy gave her back a sense of self-control. The next day when I went into her room I told her that I had forgotten to take my magic underwear off when I took a bath and that I had to hang them on the magic clothesline until they dried off. Using the idea of magic underwear started us using images for other things. She had a magic cape that she would wear to endure the painful chemotherapy procedures and when she had a "belly oowie," she'd wrap the magic cape around her stomach.

"She had fantasies in which her Cabbage Patch dolls could do all the things she couldn't do. They rode magic carpets and slid down banisters. They went to visit Mr. and Mrs. Santa at Christmas time. She was able to move between fantasy and reality easily and the fantasy world did wonders for her.

"Different kids need different things. Some just need distractions. The older kids need to talk about what was happening to them and the younger kids often use a doll or a puppet to displace their feelings. We have some books about kids dying and some of them need to talk about illness and death through the characters in the story. I watch the soaps with one 13-year-old girl. We talk about life issues in a displaced way. In one of the programs, a man is being poisoned by his nephew, who was trying to frame the wife. The man was losing his coordination and had amnesia. We talked about his body betraying him.

"'Gee,' I said to my client, 'I wonder what it's like for him.' She said it was scary and confusing but that it was a story and that, in the end, he would be all right. There was a sadness in her voice and she seemed to be saying that he'd be all right, but she didn't know if she would be."

Having had cancer seems to help Jenkins contact

the more tender aspects of the human condition. A slight woman with long brown hair and huge expressive eyes, she makes everyone she touches feel safe and listened to.

Jenkins' own ordeal began two days after she turned 15, while she was watching *Ben*, a horror movie about rats, with her cousin. "I knew something wasn't right. My hair was long and I pushed a strand back and [my fingers] hit a bump, a growth between my shoulder and neck. My aunt and uncle called my father who took me to the emergency room. They said there were five things it might be and that tests were needed.

"Over the next week, I saw several doctors. One doctor said it was a congenital gill. Another shined a light on it and said if it was cancerous you couldn't see any light through it. Since you could see light through this tumor, it wasn't bad. Nobody seemed to panic. My best friend, however, said it looked like cancer, but my mother quickly said that wasn't possible. The denial on the part of my family was wonderful because I wasn't afraid.

"When I woke up from surgery, my parents weren't there. Something seemed wrong about that. The doctor came in and told me the tumor was Hodgkin's disease, a disease of the lymph nodes. He never used the word cancer. He said the surgeon had gotten 98 percent of it but was unable to get the last bit because it was laying over my lung. He said I'd have to be in another hospital, Sloan Kettering, for a couple of weeks of treatment. He just spilled it out in a straightforward manner. I felt relieved because I knew what I had and because there was another hospital that would take care of it.

"When I got to Sloan Kettering hospital the sign said, 'Toward the conquest of cancer and allied diseases.' I figured I had an allied disease. I saw kids who had cancer and they looked thin and sick and bald. They looked weird. Since I thought I had an allied disease, I felt separated from them. I also felt blank and empty. Maybe I was in shock.

"They had teen pizza parties and lunches in the

playroom, but I never went. I didn't want to socialize with people with cancer because that would be too much like having it too. My roommate was a little boy who was very sick and who cried all the time. I asked to have him removed from the room, because he was sicker than me and he frightened me. I really built a wall around myself. A social worker kept coming by to see me, but I wouldn't talk to her. I told her I wasn't like the kids with cancer, the kids who were going to die, and that I was going to be fine. She kept coming back to talk and eventually I threw a *TV Guide* at her. My mother was mortified, but I was glad because she never came back.

"They told me they were going to have to take my spleen out because it was one of the first places invaded by the disease. There were also some diagnostic findings suggesting that there might be involvement in the lymph nodes in my groin and stomach. They also told me I'd be getting radiation and maybe chemotherapy depending on how far it had spread. If I got chemotherapy, my hair would fall out. I was really scared then. I cried a lot. My parents told me that they would get me the best wig in the world, but it didn't help.

"They told me the surgical scar would be about two inches. But when I woke up there was this long bandage running down my stomach and I told the nurse it was a large bandage for a two-inch scar. That's when she told me it was about ten inches. I hadn't been expecting that. But my mother also told me the disease hadn't spread so I didn't have to have chemo. This helped me deal with the ten-inch scar.

"My mother was with me all day. She knitted an afghan which, when completed, was the size of two king-size beds. That's how she bound her anxiety. My dad came after work and stayed until Johnny Carson was over. My stepmother, stepfather and grandmother also spent a lot of time with me.

"I started to get better and began to anticipate discharge. The medical resident came to talk about my experience and to help me explain to the kids at school what had happened to me. She asked me what I knew about my illness. I said I had Hodgkin's disease and chronicled a lot of things about it in a manner much like in a medical journal. She said I was right but that I was wrong about one thing—that Hodgkin's disease was a kind of cancer.

My whole body stopped. I couldn't do anything. She kept talking, but I didn't hear her. I just focused on the word 'cancer.' I started crying. No one had told me I had cancer. From that moment on I felt that I wasn't the same person, that [the disease] would always be with me and that I would always be different in some way. Before, I thought I had this allied disease that I'd get over.

"After the talk, a friend from school came to visit me. I felt so much older and different than her. Cancer had become very graphic to me. I had one roommate in the hospital who was always vomiting and had these huge, painful mouth sores. She was bald and very thin and if that's what cancer looked like, I didn't want any part of it. I cried when my mother came and I asked her why she didn't tell me that I had cancer. She said, 'We didn't want you to get scared.' I asked her if there was anything else people hadn't told me. She said no, but I wasn't sure I could believe her.

"I started radiation treatments before I left the hospital. They used red magic markers to indicate the field of radiation on my chest and back and they tattooed center points for the radiation field on my throat. After discharge, during the last four weeks of treatment, I stayed with my grandmother who lived closer to the hospital than my parents. During the treatments they exposed my chest and I was very uncomfortable because male personnel were there. After a while I developed a passive resignation—this was the way it had to be.

"My sisters took part in a study that was investigating various sibling characteristics and when they came to the hospital I was afraid to see them. I hadn't seen them for a number of weeks and I didn't know what they knew. My hair had fallen out in the back and I had lost 25 pounds. I was down to 90 pounds.

"I woke up feeling nauseous that day and told my mother that I was sick and I didn't want to have the treatment that day. I said I'd have it the next day instead and that I would still have the required four a week, but that I was too sick that day. She insisted. I thought I would throw up while they were radiating me. I was worried that then other areas of my body would also be radiated. When they did my back I was worried that I'd throw up and suffocate. Somehow I got out of the treatment room and threw up all over the waiting room in front of many people. My sisters freaked out. When my mother came up to me I told her, 'See, I told you I was going to be sick.' There were parts of being sick that she and the doctors couldn't control or know as well as I did.

"They kept saying, 'It's shrinking, it's shrinking, it's gone.' I didn't have to have the sixteenth radiation treatment.

"I think the hardest part of the whole thing was when I went back to school. I wanted to be normal and I couldn't be. I didn't have stamina and I didn't look good. I was told by the doctors not to go in the sun or be exposed to chlorine. I also had to stay away from alcohol, cigarettes and any drugs. The other kids were all experimenting with those things. I had just moved to a new school a month before I got sick so it was hard to fit in. The first day I was back this boy came up to me and said, 'You're the new kid. I heard you were dead.' By then I knew I was going to be okay so it didn't bother me, although I hoped 'cancer' would not become my nickname.

"How have I changed because of the ordeal? I value life a lot more. My husband tells me I make a big deal over holidays. I'm more emotional around my birthday, partly because I got sick so close to my birthday and partly because I'm glad to be around to celebrate.

"I look forward to the day that I'll be so old and walking so slow that I'll stop traffic. When I had cancer I had blocked off the idea that I might die, but now that

I'm older the full impact and seriousness of my experience is much clearer to me.

"Sometimes when I hear people complain about things, I feel they don't have their priorities right. In the grand scheme of things what they are upset about isn't very important.

"Before I got sick I wanted to be a psychologist. But I didn't want to help kids with cancer. While I was nearing the end of graduate school I heard about a camp in Maine for kids who had cancer. I didn't know if working there would be a good idea for me. It might be too close to home.

"I went and it was cathartic. I encountered the affect I didn't feel before. When the kids talked I felt they were telling my story.

"I felt that God gave me a second chance and I wanted to do something with it. I felt a need to go to church. I was grateful. I felt awe and I needed to make sense of life.

"Then last year I had some thyroid problems and I panicked. I thought the cancer had returned. My internist said that in his heart of hearts he didn't believe that it was cancer, but given my history, he had to do tests. After the first tests, my horrible fears were not realized but I still couldn't believe it. I was a basket case. I couldn't enjoy good times. I couldn't plan. I couldn't sleep.

"I felt all the things I should have felt when I was 15. I felt scared. My body was betraying me and I felt frightened and out of control. I anticipated losses and felt sad. When it was all over, I was upset with myself for losing the faith.

"My doctor asked me questions about the treatment I had back then and I realized how little I knew. All the way through the diagnostic work-up, I thought about how my illness guided what kind of person I've become, what choices I've made and my priorities.

"This sounds like a cliché, but I want to live life to the fullest. I took extra graduate courses because I wanted to explore everything. I refuse to be pigeonholed. I'm a child psychologist, which is as much as I'll allow myself to be categorized. I don't want to be limited or cut off in any way."

This same philosophy helps Donna Jenkins help kids. She knows an illness can be limiting and she tries to contact the part of the person beyond the illness. "When kids have cancer, sometimes it's hard for them to work through developmental issues. The task of an adolescent is to separate from the family and to develop an individual identity. Being sick and dependent on parents and strangers makes this difficult. There are also pubertal changes that have to be adjusted to and it's hard to develop a good body image when you are losing your hair, losing weight and have huge mouth sores. I help them hook up how difficult these tasks are with their illness and help normalize how difficult it is for them to feel good about their bodies.

"Some kids think they got sick because they were bad: 'Last summer I kicked my brother,' or 'I broke something.' The younger they are the more egocentric they are and the more they believe they can bring something horrible upon themselves. As they get older they look for more external causes, like contagion. Someone in their neighborhood had leukemia. They look for causes to make the world orderly and less scary.

"When I was considering the training position here at Dana Farber Cancer Institute, I had concerns about helping these really sick kids, kids that might die. It's difficult and I sometimes become emotionally exhausted. I'm more in touch with anger and sadness and premature loss. I need to rely on my faith, my belief that things happen for a reason and that although life's events can be unfair and horrible, I believe that in the grand scheme of things, life does make some sense.

"I have to let go of my need for control. I have to let go and accept the uncertainties, however bad they are. I try not to concentrate on the fact that a child may die. I try to appreciate where we are now and to explore the feelings in the moment. I try to remember that there is a person in there separate from the disease and I try to experience that person.

Donna Jenkins imparts a critical message: "The most important thing these kids need to know is that *they* have the disease. The disease *does not* have them." Clearly, this is something she herself has learned, enabling her to live life to its fullest.

Reverend Jeb Magruder

Honesty is important to Jeb Stuart Magruder. He learned the hard way just how damaging his own dishonesty was, not only because of the searing effect it had on his self-worth, but also because of its effect on his reputation as a public figure. Ultimately, Magruder was imprisoned for his supervisory role in the Watergate cover-up and his subsequent perjury while under oath during the hearings.

In 1971 Jeb Magruder, deputy director of communications in the Nixon White House, was asked to direct the operations of Richard Nixon's presidential re-election campaign and to be Nixon's "special assistant." He was highly regarded for his planning and marketing expertise and succeeded in making Nixon's 1972 campaign extremely effective. However, unknown by the public at the time was the fact that the campaign went far beyond clever marketing and publicity strategies to include completely illegal tactics.

In June 1972, a team of five men with wiretapping equipment broke into the offices of Larry O'Brien and the Democratic National Committee at the Watergate office-apartment complex in Washington, D.C. When the men were arrested, Attorney General John Mitchell assigned

Jeb Magruder to keep the prosecutors, the press and the general public from connecting the Watergate break-in to the President's re-election campaign.

As the campaign's misconduct began to leak, Magruder followed Mitchell's suggestion and burned the burglary plan—called the "Gemstone" file—in his living room fireplace. Magruder then constructed a cover story that he and the others involved fed to the Watergate prosecutors and a federal grand jury. G. Gordon Liddy, an ex-CIA agent and counsel to the re-election committee, and E. Howard Hunt, another ex-CIA agent, along with James McCord and the four burglars, agreed to go along with Magruder's cover-up story, a story that made them the "fall" guys. They were all indicted. Magruder was not. In fact, he directed Nixon's second inauguration in January 1973 and received high acclaim for the job he did.

A few days after the inauguration, Magruder lied at the trial of Hunt, Liddy, and McCord and the four burglars. Just before he was to be sentenced, McCord began to talk, hoping that he would receive a shorter sentence. As the story began to break down, Magruder got scared and hired several lawyers, anticipating the problems that were soon to tear his world apart. Not quite certain about how bad the situation was, he lied to the lawyers, telling them the cover-up story instead of the truth.

Sensing that Magruder was lying, one of them said, "Jeb, pretty soon you're going to have to tell the truth." It did not take Magruder long to agree with them; the very next day he came clean and on April 13, 1973 he pleaded guilty to a felony charge of conspiracy to obstruct justice.

As Magruder explained, "I felt a tremendous sense of relief; I felt almost happy to be finished with the cover-up and all its lies. I felt as if I'd been seized by a madness for a long time and suddenly I had become sane again." John Long explains in the book *Sources of Inspiration* that ten months before, when Magruder burned the burglary plans in his fireplace, he had wondered if his life too would go up in smoke. And now, by telling the truth, he felt that perhaps he was beginning to rise up from those ashes.

Magruder said he had asked for and received God's forgiveness and was now willing to accept punishment for his illegal activities. He seemed extremely credible to the court and he received wide approval for his straightforward testimony during the Senate Watergate hearings. Clearly, this was an important turning point for Magruder.

Magruder's comeback has been long and difficult, but he persevered. After serving a prison term for his role in the Watergate events, he returned to graduate school, earned a master's degree in divinity at Princeton Theological Seminary in 1981, endured a painful divorce, worked through a serious clinical depression, started over again in a new marriage and a new career and worked his way up to become a senior minister.

Magruder is the first to acknowledge that he was able to gain from and overcome his incredibly dramatic trauma in large part because of the help and forgiveness of others. For example, in October 1988—after the door of an armored truck opened and spilled millions of dollars onto a freeway in Ohio, and an estimated 200 people tore out of their cars to grab as many bills as they could— Mayor Dana G. Rinehart and other community leaders decided to form the Columbus Commission on Ethics as a means of encouraging citizens to examine the value of ethics in their lives.

Jeb Stuart Magruder, then executive minister of the First Community Church in Columbus, was appointed chairman of this committee. Mayor Rinehart felt that the lessons Magruder had learned from Watergate made him a natural choice to lead the panel of business, education and religious leaders. Not everyone, however, agreed with the mayor's choice. Indeed, many believed that after Watergate, Jeb Magruder should have had the decency never to show his face in public again.

In 1990, Magruder won the overwhelmingly positive endorsement of others when he was chosen over 277 other applicants to become senior minister of the First

Presbyterian Church of Lexington, Kentucky. The vote by secret ballot of 254 to 5 showed that the congregation forgave him for his lapse of ethics in Watergate. As one person on the nomination committee remarked, "If you can't forgive people, you ought not to be in the church to start with." It is interesting to note that while Magruder played a large part in his own fall, it did not prevent others from giving him a second chance. Indeed, were it not for their forgiveness and willingness to allow Magruder to come clean, there is a good chance that he would not be where he is today.

With every step back from the Watergate scandal, Magruder has been the target of abuse, anger and skepticism. When he toured the country promoting his first book, *An American Life: One Man's Road to Watergate*, written in the months prior to imprisonment, he noticed something he mentions in his second book, *From Power to Peace*—that religious conversions of celebrity sinners invite skepticism. As Long suggests in his chapter in *Sources of Inspiration*, Magruder's story was not so outrageously ironic as were those of television evangelists Jim Bakker and Jimmy Swaggart who hailed themselves as moral leaders when they fell.

Interestingly, Magruder's involvement with religion did not start suddenly after Watergate when he needed help. Indeed, Magruder was an altar boy at an Episcopalian church, even though his parents, who were Presbyterians, did not attend their own church very frequently. When he was a young teenager he was a faithful churchgoer and while attending Williams College, he had many lengthy talks with the chaplain and teacher of ethics about right and wrong. Later, Magruder became a Presbytcrian elder and his family went to church regularly. The main difference between his attitude toward religion before and after Watergate was that he had kept religion separate from the rest of his life.

Magruder says that his religious awakening after Watergate was far more intense than any of his earlier experiences with the church. He says that his understanding of and dedication to Christianity started to germinate while he waited for sentencing and that it intensified significantly while he was in prison, a place that offered him the most extreme vision of human suffering he had yet to encounter. In fact, it was during his imprisonment that Magruder decided that God wanted him to help other people.

Magruder remembers when he was given a lie detector test by an FBI agent who asked him if he'd received any of the Nixon re-election campaign money. He recalls the exchange:

"I don't see how that's related to the cover-up."

"Will you answer the question, Jeb?"

"I don't want to."

"Why not?"

"It's irrelevant."

"You're not telling the truth. Come on, now. How much did you get?"

Magruder didn't want to answer because he had some expense funds left over from campaign bills which he had planned to use for his legal expenses. John Mitchell had assured him the campaign would pay for his legal expenses, but was vague about just how it would work. Magruder reasoned that his legal costs would be legitimate campaign expenses.

The FBI agent told the prosecutors that Magruder would not divulge any information regarding the money and he was eventually pressured into returning it. One of the prosecutors said, "Well, we know you took the $7000, so who knows what else you are hiding. We know you aren't telling the truth and we know you can't help it. It's just the way you are." Then came the head-shaking and the cold, disapproving eyes and arrogant smiles.

During the Watergate hearings, when the media declared him to be one of the "most hated men in America" and afterward when he was ignored, abandoned, misunderstood and punished, Magruder took an honest look at himself and didn't like what he saw. He felt that he had traded his soul for a piece of the action. He felt that he had failed to adhere to his ethical principles because he'd become obsessed with an ambition, that his quest for power had overshadowed his integrity. Magruder says that he does not want to forget that he went to prison and that he lost control of his life, because it was through shame and self-reflection that he was able to recover a life of integrity.

In *Sources of Inspiration,* Long quotes Magruder as telling Senator Joseph Montoya, one of the interrogators during the Watergate hearings: "I am not going to lay down and die because of this. I think I will rehabilitate myself.... I think I am in that process and I hope to be able to live a useful life. I would not recommend this as a method of re-emergence, but in this case, I think I can and I will."

Even though he wanted to turn to a life of religious honesty, Magruder questioned whether God still loved him and whether He would forgive him. Just after testifying before the Ervin Committee, Magruder received a letter from Reverend Louis Evans and his wife Colleen, of the National Presbyterian Church. "We feel a special empathy with you," they wrote. "I think we understand something of where you have been and where you are trying to go—because we have seen God use other painful circumstances to offer His love and show us that He can bring goodness out of disaster."

Through Louis Evans, whom he calls "Louie," Magruder was introduced to a spiritual community. Evans invited Magruder to join a men's Bible-study group and this became a major support for him, both while he was awaiting sentencing and while he was in prison. It was then that he felt "the love of God transmitted through one human being to another." Whereas the prosecutors seemed to consider themselves to be moral judges, Magruder's Christian friends were concerned about the pain he was experiencing. More than anything else, their concern gave Magruder the strength and determination he needed to survive. It seemed that while his own strength was being drained, he was being transfused with the strength of others. Reverend Evans played a major role in Magruder's ability to believe that God forgave him. Evans told him that if he accepted God, God would accept him and offer his forgiveness. Magruder later wrote, "I found myself speaking to Christ as if he were in the car with us.... I had never spoken to him so directly. Magruder says that he "would give my life to Christ... if he would accept me." Exuberantly, Magruder told Evans that God said "it was okay!"

In 1989, Magruder appeared on Joan Lunden's talk show with psychologist Dr. Herbert Saltzstein and Dr. Ernest van den Haz, an ethics professor. In front of a live audience and many television cameras, they discussed the issue of lying.

Magruder was introduced by Joan Lunden as an "honesty expert" who had learned his lessons from Watergate. "Honesty is usually the best policy," Magruder said. It seemed ironic that television now was painting Magruder as someone who only told the truth when 15 years ago he was viewed as someone who only lied.

Lunden, in an orange suit, swept into the audience on black spike heels, soundless on the pink carpet of the stage set. She went into the audience and approached a woman. "How much do you weigh?" she asked her. Then, holding the microphone at a man, she asked, "How much do you earn?" Turning to the panel she asked, "Do little white lies lead to bigger ones? What should we teach our children about lying?"

I interviewed Magruder at the airport after the taping of the show. A young employee of the television station drove us there—past the threshing motors of buses, through the shimmer of fumes and noise of 747 jets. The driver was in grade school during the Watergate scandal and had never heard of Jeb Stuart Magruder.

"How long you been a minister?" the kid asked.

"Eight years," Magruder answered.

"What'd you do before that?"

"Politics."

"Huh? That's sort of a strange switch, isn't it?"

"Yes," Magruder answered. "I was so successful in politics, I quit."

Magruder and I talked in the airport's lounge. His manner was less cautious and more serene than it was during the Watergate hearings that were now almost two decades ago. He wore thin-rimmed glasses and when trying to clarify his thoughts, he gripped the left lens between thumb and forefinger and held it as if to bring things into focus. His eyes—a brilliant blue—were the most vivid part of his appearance. But it was not just their color. More striking was his gaze when he looked at me earnestly. Magruder's voice was earnest, too, full of vigor and resonance. "When I got to the White House my dreams were much more secular," he said. "I was an upwardly mobile young man. I went to good schools, but I had to work hard to get there. My father, who was a wonderful man, had never really done well. I had to scrape to get through Williams College and the University of Chicago where I got my MBA.

"I got to the White House when I was 34. I was a good organizer and a good motivator and I had previously run Nixon's campaign in Southern California. I got to the White House because I knew key people in California, which was Nixon's home base.

"I had dreams of running for office myself, but running for office is an iffy proposition. I also considered being the vice president of a big corporation, a Clark Clifford of the Nixon Administration. Clifford worked out at the same club as I did and I thought he had a pretty nice life. I wanted to contribute to society and to be of service, but another motive in my life was to be in a position of power and influence.

"Just before Watergate broke I was executive chairman of the inaugural. I was a very important person and determined who sat where at the balls, concerts and dinners. Everybody loved me. I had control over the cars, the limos and the drivers, so in that sense I was quite popular."

Quickly his mood became pensive. "I thought I'd have an important role in the next four years, but in March [when Watergate broke], most of my friends took off. Nobody would touch me during that disaster. They were afraid of guilt by association and they were afraid they'd be indicted. I felt terrible.

"Up until March I was on top of the world. Then all of a sudden I was at the bottom. It was traumatic.

"When people are in crisis, a natural survival instinct takes over; they survive because they have to. During the period from 1973 to 1975 my survival instinct was pretty strong.

"I was beat to death by the press who saw me as one of the worst people in the world, so I raised my resistance to pain to a very high level. I was in Korea at the end of the war and knew something about being in a situation where you can live or die depending on what move you make. In this case it was death for my career and in a sense for my marriage, too. And it was death for the hopes and dreams I had had.

"You just steal yourself away and resist all the negatives so that they can call you anything they want to on television and you just say to yourself, 'They're wrong, so forget about them.' I used every trick in the book to manipulate the system to survive. Some of the things I ended up doing seem hilarious as I look back. Most of the prosecutors just saw me as fodder for their investigation, but one of them was empathetic. This prosecutor would pass information to a lawyer friend of mine who would pass it to me, so I was aware of what was going on. When I got into situations, I could protect myself." It was important for Magruder to find favor with Judge John Sirica, "so that I would get a break if there was any break to be given. Sirica didn't give me a break when he sentenced me; four years is a very long sentence. But then, he let me go after seven months. That is very unusual. And I think part of it was that the cooperation

I gave was understood by the judge. He didn't like what I had done, but he was favorably impressed by who I was personally.

"When Archibald Cox was the prosecutor, he was absolutely vindictive. For example, my father-in-law couldn't go to Europe because my mother-in-law was sick, so he offered me and my wife the trip. He said, Take the tickets, fly over to Greece and take a break from all the hassle.' We appreciated this because we couldn't afford to do it on our own. Unfortunately, the prosecutor, Cox, had my passport. Nonchalantly, I went to see the prosecutors and asked them if I could have it. They almost died. They said, 'You are a felon. You can escape. And you are a bad person anyway. Bad people aren't allowed to do these kinds of things.' The guilt trip they gave me was unbelievable, particularly since I knew enough about them to know they weren't angels either.

"So a couple of friends of mine talked to Sirica and he knew that with my four kids in Washington I wouldn't take off.... Cox himself took the issue to the judge. He told the judge what a terrible person I was and how I might try to escape. Sirica jumped all over him. He said, 'That's ridiculous. This guy isn't any more going to take off than the man on the moon. He's been very cooperative. So what's your problem? Do you want to punish him? Are you the judge?' So I learned to use any skills I had in order to survive in the system.

"I had done something wrong, which I admitted early on, but I wasn't Genghis Khan or Attila the Hun, both of whom I had been compared to. What kept me alive or my hope alive was that I wasn't going to let people tell me who I was."

Magruder feels that he was guilty of having a tremendous insensitivity to the basic tenets of democracy. The consequences of his own wiretapping activities hit home after his friends, John Dean, Bob Haldeman and John Ehrlichman secretly taped conversations that they had with him. "I went into a rage. Those were *private talks*. They had no *right* to do that. Finally I realized, not just intellectually, but also in my gut, that we had no right to wiretap Larry O'Brien's phone either. Nor, I eventually came to see, can society tolerate the act of perjury, which strikes at the heart of our justice system.

"Dirty tricks are not an appropriate way to deal in politics, but political parties have been doing it forever. Most of Watergate was a series of dirty tricks. Laughable, almost, as were some of Kennedy's dirty tricks in the 1960s. No question, we got out of hand, but we were treated as if we were the arch villains of all times. Part of the reason was that Nixon was hated by the press and the 'liberal establishment' and that certainly affected what happened to us."

The Watergate fiasco happened, according to Jeb Magruder, because Richard Nixon and the people who were working for him considered themselves to be surrounded by liberal enemies—in the media, the Congress and in the academic world—and they felt they had to get their enemies before the enemies got them. In Nixon's case, concepts from war were transferred to politics. The conceptual system of war encompasses destroying the enemy, with the means justifying the end. The atmosphere in the White House was highly charged and encouraged a siege mentality. Those around Nixon (whose nickname when on Air Force One was Searchlight) lacked any independent vision that might have helped them avoid mistakes. Magruder, in hindsight, views press secretary Ron Ziegler, a former Disneyland guide, as scarcely more than a "ventriloquist's dummy." Magruder says that White House counsel Chuck Colson would say whatever the President wanted to hear and he also encouraged Nixon's darker side, his instinct to go for the jugular.

When Magruder first arrived at the White House, he remembers that one of the network correspondents showed an anti-administration bias. As a result, Nixon immediately called him a communist. "Jeb, you're our new ramrod around here," Nixon said, "get the word out on that guy." Magruder notes, "I didn't waste time soul searching. I'd already seen that the assistants who tried to second-guess the President's judgments didn't last long.... There just wasn't any room for debate."

One time Magruder disagreed with Haldeman's instructions to send letters and telegrams blasting certain senators for opposing the President. Haldeman wrote back in a memo, "This is pure BS...and besides, this was an order, not a question." When Nixon was criticized for bombing Hanoi, Chuck Colson suggested running an advertisement that accused the President's critics of treason.

In this atmosphere it is easy to see how someone like G. Gordon Liddy was hired to handle the gathering of intelligence. When Liddy outlined his plan to use mugging squads, kidnapping, sabotage, prostitutes and break-ins, both John Dean and Magruder were stunned. But no one, including Magruder, objected or worried about the illegality of the plan. The only suggestion was made by Attorney General John Mitchell who told Liddy to "tone [the plan] down" because the financial cost was too high.

According to Magruder, a toned-down version of Liddy's plan was approved pretty easily "because of the climate of fear and suspicion that had developed in the White House. This suspicious attitude started with the President and filtered down to us through Haldeman, Colson and others. It came to affect all of our thinking so decisions that at the time seemed rational now seem insane...somehow they then seemed acceptable, perhaps because we were discussing these decisions in the office of the Attorney General of the United States."

An illusion of absolute power operated in the cover-up. Magruder says, "It seemed inconceivable that with our political power we could not erase the mistakes we had made." The men involved told themselves they were protecting the President and persuaded themselves that what they had done, although technically illegal, was not wrong or unusual and that their enemies were simply making a mountain out of a molehill. The Watergate affair was not discussed in terms of perjury or burglary or conspiracy, but in terms of "handling the case" and "making sure things don't get out of hand." The attitude was that "we were not covering up a burglary, we were safeguarding world peace."

Magruder realized that before Watergate he had been so ambitious that he became self-centered. He realized, too, that he'd always had a feeling of restlessness. "Something wasn't quite right about wherever I was or whatever I was doing. I was never really happy, even though I had everything supposedly necessary to make a person happy." He had always felt that the next step up the ladder would provide him with what was missing in his life, but it never did. When all his worldly supports disappeared, he began to realize how flimsy these "supports" really were. He realized that what was missing was a relationship with God.

When Louie Evans asked him to minister to others, Magruder began to realize that everything in his life had not been wiped out by Watergate. "Something good was left. The fact that Louie could forgive me and see good in me revived something that I thought was long dead within me: a small measure of self-respect."

After pleading guilty, Magruder was sent to Allenwood, a minimum-security prison in Pennsylvania. He felt that the people who ran the prison were completely ignorant of what went on inside.

"When I got to Allenwood, I realized I was really in very deep trouble. There were many instances of rape and violence. I knew the other prisoners didn't like me and it was just a matter of time before something would happen. You can't really protect yourself, at least not for prolonged periods of time. Minimum security was actually much worse than maximum because you can't just go into a cell and close the door. So, God must have been at work here. After I'd been there a week, Johnny Sample arrived. He was a black ex-cornerback with the New York Jets who was one of the toughest players of all times. He was in prison for passing bad checks. He was a super athlete and a good tennis player. I was the only other person in the prison who could play tennis and give him a reasonable match. So, literally, he and I made a deal. I'd play tennis with him and he'd protect me. And that worked. I was sure I would have been attacked sooner or later, so I had to figure out how to survive one way or another.

"Depression dogged me all of the time. I don't think it was ever so pervasive that I couldn't function, but I had all the standard symptoms of serious depression—sleeping too much, or not sleeping at all, feeling a lot of anxiety, having night-sweats, waking up with 'if-only' thoughts, worrying about all kinds of things, most of which I couldn't do anything about anyway. I had feelings of total hopelessness. There wasn't any place to go.

"The depression became even worse after I got out of prison, because I had no job. You finally made it through and you were out. You're ready to start over and you're free, but it's different. You are no longer the young MBA graduate known as a great political organizer. You are now Jeb Stuart Magruder, an ex-Watergate convict. I realized that this incident would stick with me for the rest of my life. I thought maybe I should change my name or leave the country. Clearly, I was no longer a sought-after commodity.

"When I began to look for work I went to this guy who was a recruiter and who had been a wonderful friend of mine before Watergate. He agreed to meet me for breakfast and I brought my résumé with me. I said, 'Ed, I'd like to get back into business now. I paid my penalty.' He then chewed me out for an hour and told me what a lowlife I was, that I had betrayed the country and that he wouldn't think of lowering himself to help me.

"What was so infuriating is that he had set me up. I called him saying that I wanted to get back into the retail business and he said, 'Yeah, let's have breakfast.' Then he spent an hour telling me what a bad person I was.

"So, I started to separate out different kinds of

people—those who were compassionate and forgiving and those who were not."

When Magruder's first book, *An American Life*, came out in paperback, he went on a publicity tour during which he encountered skepticism from his audience about his religious conversion. "How can you claim to be a Christian after committing such a serious crime?" reporters asked. It angered Magruder to be viewed as a hypocrite and a charlatan, so he quit halfway through the tour.

The publicity tour had made him feel like he was running in circles; he wanted to be home to deal with critical family issues. After 23 years, his marriage was ending. "It took a long time. I think one reason that the divorce happened was because Gail had to pay a penalty even though she hadn't done anything. Marriage is at best a fragile institution anyway and when you throw in issues like going to prison when the wife hasn't done anything, it takes its toll.

"After the divorce was over, I started to climb back up, slowly getting the feeling that I could survive again. It took a long, long time to succeed. After that awful breakfast with the recruiter, I found some business opportunities, but I chose to go with Young Life, a religious organization that worked with high school kids. That was a very nice job. I chose to go with Young Life not necessarily because of its religious connotations or because I had some deep abiding understanding of the value of what Young Life did by helping kids and wanting to be a part of it, but I wanted to be in a place that would be safe, where I wasn't going to be crucified every day as I might have been in the commercial world. It was a self-protective move.

"Unfortunately, however, Young Life ended up not being all that safe, but it wasn't their fault. There's a tendency to get ex-sinners out front for evangelical groups, so I gave my testimony on the banquet circle for them. That's how they raise money. Ollie North went through that and was supported by Jerry Falwell. I got involved with some of those people. So for three years, from 1975 to 1978, I bounced around the country regurgitating my past to others. I was always going back; I wasn't going forward. I was like a freak at a carnival. 'Here's this guy. Look at him and he'll tell you how to come back from whatever.'

' "But it wasn't really helpful to me. I felt I was being used. Not in a bad way; people weren't consciously saying, 'Let's figure out how to exploit this person,' but that's what it felt like. A lot of it was my own guilt feelings. I still felt guilty about all the things that had happened, but repeating the stories became very harmful.

"I had a lot of anxiety at this time. I felt exploited and felt that I, too, was exploiting people. 'Come see this Watergate guy and he'll help you find God.' I felt that God didn't want me to do this. I think God talks to us in different ways and when you start doing something that makes you feel uncomfortable, that's a good indication that it's not what God wants you to do.

"So in 1978, having taken classes in conjunction with Young Life at Fuller Seminary in California, I decided to go to Princeton which was a leading Presbyterian seminary. My father had gone to Princeton University and I had lived 40 miles from Princeton when I was a youngster. Our family used to go to all the football games. It was natural for me to go to the seminary there."

At Princeton, Magruder worked with Reverend James Loder, author of *The Transforming Moment: Understanding Convictional Experiences*, a book about sudden life-changing bursts of religious knowledge that come during a crisis. Loder encourages people to remember the times when they have lost control of their lives because those moments transcend the horizons of ordinary thinking and disclose an ultimate reality.

Loder himself had such an experience in 1970 when he stopped on the road to help a woman who had a flat tire. As he was changing her flat, another car hit the car he was working on, which then rolled on top of him. After this life-threatening experience, Loder began teaching in a much more personal way. According to Magruder, "Rather than playing the role of the intellectual professor teaching theology at an aloof stance from his students, Loder got in there with you to deal with real theology in your own life and how you apply that in different settings." Magruder identified with Loder because they had both been ultra logical and rational, before certain life experiences taught them the meaning of faith.

In 1982, Magruder was ordained and became an associate Presbyterian minister in Burlingame, California. A year later his wife left him and he was despondent, but was helped by numerous supportive friends. Then, in 1984, just after he moved to Ohio, as executive minister of another church, he became severely depressed, but no longer had a network of nearby friends to help him.

"Psychotherapy helped me understand that I was actually okay. I had been depressed for such a long time that I wondered if I would be that way for the rest of my life. I thought I might be mentally ill. Therapy helped me understand that what I was feeling was a normal reaction to the many losses and problems I had experienced. I also understood that the only person who could solve my problems was me. Antidepressant drugs, which help many people, wouldn't work on me.

"I learned that what I could do with my life, although it wasn't as important in the world's eyes as what I did before, was equally important. I could make a difference by participating in the ministry. I always believed that political problems should be solved at a local level, one neighbor helping another. I began to look at my job in a positive way.

"I began to realize, too, that there was life after divorce. At one point I didn't think there was. I realized there was potential in the relationship I had with Patti Newton, an educator and counselor who later became my second wife.

"Therapy helped me understand that I needed to have roots. I needed to feel at home somewhere. So, in

Ohio I began to participate in the community. It took me awhile, but I even began to see the Ohio State football team as my team.

"Another way I felt part of the community was through participating in church activities. We fed the homeless every Monday night. As a minister I helped people in crisis, people who had a death in their family, who had lost their jobs or who had been through a divorce. I could contribute as much because of my experience as anything else. All my losses began to become positive.

"The ministry was the best place for me to be. I had an opportunity to work out my own issues while helping people work out theirs. Had I done what some of my Watergate colleagues did—go into business—I might not have been able to work through the pain of what had happened to me. I recovered because I dealt with my problems directly—and because God became the center of my life.

"The church community is a perfect place for somebody trying to recover in life because it is a caring community and understanding about such things as depression.

"My spiritual journey was also helpful. Acceptance of me goes beyond human acceptance. As a minister, my job is to make the life of Jesus Christ meaningful and make it translate to help people today, to help them with their issues. Jesus' life was not a glory-filled life, in a secular sense.... Life is difficult and not always fair. In spite of that, there is always hope. No matter how things are today, half of the gospel message is that there's hope for tomorrow, as we understand our relationship with a transcendent God. That became meaningful for me as I began to deal with my own depression.

"Heaven and hell are here now. In the Christian faith we've always believed in life after death, but we also believe in the present. Depending on how you live your life, heaven and hell are here now. Jesus Christ's message is not only about the future, it's about today. Jesus said to the prostitute, the woman at the well, 'Go and sin no more.' She had this sinful life, but there was hope for her. He offered that to the tax collector and all the other negative people in that society. Jesus said, 'Come and follow me and you'll have a new life.' That's a much more important part of the Christian message than the one about salvation in the afterlife.

"If you have a conflictual relationship with somebody, that's hell. There was someone on the staff in Columbus who I clashed with for the first year. Then we said, 'Isn't this ridiculous?' We had things in common, but our egos clashed. Beyond that, he had value as a person. There's a dimension of faith that enables us to transcend personal differences, our egos and self-interest."

Mostly, people seem to have forgiven Magruder. "I've found very little intolerance—not to say there aren't some cynics around." When Magruder was chosen to lead the ethics commission, Mike Turner of Columbus wrote a letter to the Columbus *Dispatch* which appeared on their editorial page. "I remember Magruder as the most facile and convincing liar of the Watergate hearings." Magruder's appointment, Turner wrote, "embarrasses our city." Turner felt that the mayor should "distinguish fame from infamy and perhaps irony from absurdity."

A member of Magruder's church, Wilamine Wykle, was angered by Turner's letter and wrote in Magruder's defense, "He is a conscientious and devout student of the Bible. We who are touched by his teachings have no doubt that God has long since forgiven him for his part in the Watergate scandal." She added that she doubted that Turner was a "sin-free person."

Reverend Edsel Ammons, bishop of the United Methodist Church of Western Ohio, added, "I can't think of anyone better to help us look at these questions. If anybody knows to what extremes people can go, Jeb certainly does. He can be a bell-ringer for us."

In October 1990, when Magruder left Columbus for a position as senior minister of the First Presbyterian

Church, the Columbus *Dispatch* wrote that he had become a "respected civic leader" and that the city would miss him.

"I'm a safe person for people to go to," Magruder explains. "They think, 'Hey, he's been through a lot, so he'll understand my problems.' Ministers are the first line of professional help and I don't have my own agenda. I'm not trying to get another job or make more money. I don't owe anybody.

"In politics there's always the quid pro quo. You are always paying someone off for favors. Now I do things on my terms rather than on somebody else's. My loyalties are to a higher power."

Magruder says the one other thing that helped him recover was something he learned from his mother. "Never give up." He says that many successful people have come to the same conclusion. "It's what Churchill said, 'Never, never, never, never give up.' Six words."

Deena Metzger

Although Deena Metzger is a poet, novelist and playwright, she may be best known for the poster portraying the nude upper part of her body after she had a mastectomy. With her arms stretched to the sky, she reveals the tree limb that she had tattooed over the scar on the flat area of her chest where her breast used to be.

Metzger now counsels other people with serious and life-threatening diseases and has published two books, *Writing for Your Life: A Guide and Companion to the Inner Worlds* and *Tree*, an account of her fight with and ultimate victory over cancer.

On February 5, 1977, Deena Metzger learned that she had breast cancer. She knew that she could not have her health back just because she wanted it, yet she felt there was something she could do to help herself. If she could create harmony where there was war, if she could exhume and revitalize what was being taken away, if she could transform what limited her, then she would have a better chance of living.

In her poem "Between the Worlds," Metzger asks:

> Flesh like metal
> Spirit like mist
> teach me the gait

151

of the luminous wolves
drinking from the dark river.
In those waters
the stones sing,
can the world
mend
in this body?

Metzger saw a connection between disease and the way she feels the American culture suppresses the life force. She reduced her activities to life-giving ones and discovered that imagination and creativity have the ability to heal. Creativity, she believes, is a gift from another realm, a gift that we can use to restore and reclaim parts of ourselves that may be lost or buried. We use this gift, Metzger feels, to integrate what has been alienated, to reconstruct a scattered self and to go beyond our furthest limits. After nurturing this gift, she feels that we can then pass it on to others.

"Creativity makes everything possible. Our bodies know this and respond to it. Early on, my intuition was that cancer is a manifestation of silences; what I had not expressed had festered within me. So, I took my typewriter to the hospital and spoke into the page; I wrote down whatever came to me. At the moment, that was what was essential to me."

In *Writing for Your Life* she quotes Gaston Bachelare, "What is the source of our first sufferings? It lies in the fact that we hesitated to speak. It was born in the moment when we accumulated silent things within us." Metzger believes that public discourses have corrupted language and she began looking for a language that did not distract or cloud, one that took her directly into herself. Revelations into inner worlds are not about consensus or prior definition. Deena says that when people really speak their minds, they are afraid they will become embarrassed or endangered. As she began to inhabit an inner world where she could really be with herself, she began to gather together pieces she thought might be the foundation of a self for her. She felt that she was participating in a vast underground or commonality that may have been with us since the beginning of time. This realm is what Carl Jung called the collective unconscious. Deena says, "[This realm] is infinite. To enter it is to come to know something of it and to learn of the boundlessness of the self."

"From there I began an exploration of voices that I hadn't paid too much attention to before. The first was the one who wanted me dead or who wanted to die." Deena discovered this voice while investigating her psyche through writing. It was a punitive and vicious voice and it began to tell her that she was no good, didn't deserve to live and that her life didn't matter.

"It was not unlike voices that many women in our society hear," Metzger says. "They don't feel entitled to fully partake and don't feel entitled to live with zest and enthusiasm. It was a hard and hateful voice which on a political level was the introjection of misogyny in our society.

"I began to wonder if the man I loved would turn away from my altered body. I remember before the cancer how I hated my body. Sixteen years ago I was 40 years old and I am an attractive woman, but I have often disliked my body. When I was younger, I suffered from bouts of anorexic-like eating behavior; I was trying to do away with myself by dieting. I took the values of our culture and our families and internalized them. This is particularly common for women. With men, the rage they feel because they don't have the right skin color or because they don't come from the right kind of family or they don't have equal opportunities shows itself in the form of outward expression. Often women tend to take the rage they feel and turn it toward themselves. Men can become violent and women can become mad.

"Once I began to hear the voices, I started to see their origins and to take a stand. I said to myself, 'This is not *of* me. This is coming *at* me. Then I realized that what was lethal to me was not lethal to me alone." Deena felt that she needed to listen, be aware and deeply feel the grief that others felt and she knew that this would take courage. "Being a warrior is one of the things I know about," she says. "A warrior takes a stand, is able to identify the death forces and is able to hold onto love and passion for life in the face of negative energies."

Deena was in such a state of shock about learning that she had cancer that she didn't ask the doctor any questions about the mastectomy before it was performed. He told her not to worry about how her body looked afterward because they would begin reconstructive surgery soon after the mastectomy. As the anesthesia began to take effect, she imagined the doctors making a sand castle on her chest, but when she woke up she was surprised to find that she was still flat as a boy. Apparently, the hospital's electricity had failed and because she'd already had anesthesia several times, she'd have to wait at least six months to have it again. It would take two years and three operations. By that time the skin would have healed so that they'd have to gradually stretch it with larger and larger implants. "I was beside myself but vanity kept me from [having reconstructive surgery]. It seemed easier to be flat on one side than to have two breasts of different sizes. Then in the course of time, while wrestling with all of this, I ran into a tattooist. That made all the difference in the world. My psyche had shifted by then. I said, 'What is wrong with my body? There's nothing wrong with it. It's just asymmetrical, that's all.'

"When I had my chest tattooed, it actually looked rather nice. I began to understand that something important had happened; I was thinking about my body more lovingly than when I had two breasts!

"When did I begin to love my body? I wanted to live and I realized that I couldn't dance without my body. Also, men were exceedingly kind. I didn't run into anyone who said, 'Oh my God, you're deformed. You are ugly.' And I had one wonderful lover, who one day as I was putting on my robe and covering myself, said, 'Why are you hunching your shoulders? Why are you hiding? You are a beautiful woman.'

"When I went to the health club after getting the tattoo women would say to me, 'Thank you.' I began to realize that I was the only woman in the club who had had a mastectomy. In other words, all the other women [who had had the operation] were hiding.

"That's when I had the idea to do the poster. I put the poster out in the world because I was feeling great about my body and was feeling healthy and alive and I wanted to communicate that to others. I felt gratitude from both men and women. Men were coming up to me and saying things like, 'You know, I have a one-in-ten chance of ending up with a lover or a wife with one breast. You've made it possible for me to contemplate being with a woman who has had a mastectomy.'

"Then when all the information came out about the danger of silicone implants, I realized that a miracle had happened. I had saved myself from having implants and I was given the opportunity to speak to women encouragingly so that they wouldn't think their lives were destroyed [if they had to have a mastectomy].

"Women often don't know they have value or are beautiful unless they meet someone else's standards. The idea of beauty as someone revealing themselves for who they are is a very foreign notion to many people.

"For me, healing was to live outside the tortures of the monoculture we live in. The torments and repressions of the culture establish themselves in our bodies, so I tried to get outside the culture and live with sensuality, sexuality and joy. In 1976 I was working for the Center for the Healing Arts, one of the first community organizations to concern itself with alternative healing methods, holistic medicine and other ways of healing. I was living in an environment where the emotional aspects of healing were understood, so when I discovered I had cancer I asked, 'What is the meaning of the illness and how can I stimulate the immune system?'

"Once I began to answer these questions, I responded in as many ways as I could. I looked for different healing alternatives. I knew it was essential to gather a community around me. I valued, meditated and contemplated what it meant to be in such a community. Because I realized how much I needed others, I opened myself up to the energy that was coming toward me. I began to think about which foods were life-giving and which foods weren't; I changed my diet quickly. In fact, I changed my whole life style so that I wasn't desperately exhausted and living according to someone else's agenda."

Metzger discovered that "healing is the painstaking process by which we create and sustain a life in which we can thrive." She worked painstakingly, one day at a time, to create a new life. "Ironically, as I moved toward healing, I began to live in the moment, choosing my actions carefully, doing what was meaningful, taking the time to love fully. I turned toward spirit in a more active way, not to calm myself, but for vision and understanding. Meditation was one way [that I did this] and embracing nature was another. I acknowledged the sacred. *Nature is sacred.* In nature, the gods are present in the world.

"About a month ago I was to give a talk on storytelling in San Francisco. I was agitated because I wasn't sure how to begin. I went out to a café and did a little meditation in which I called the four archangels. I surrounded myself with their energy and asked for a story. A few moments later an old drunk, clutching a bottle under his jacket, came into the café. He asked me for some money and I wondered if I should [oblige him] and encourage his habit. Then I realized that he had lived his whole life without my advice and I decided to give him some money. We then made eye contact and he said, 'God bless you.' I appreciated the blessing and he began to go on his way. He got as far as two tables away and turned around and said, 'Would you like to hear a story? Do you know what General Patton said when he was fighting in

North Africa? He said, Lo, though I walk through the valley of the shadow of death.' He nodded to me and walked on. Then he turned around again and looked at me very deeply and said, 'Lo, though I walk in the valley of the shadow of death.' Then he walked away and I thought, what an extraordinary experience. The man was an angel. Every culture tells the story of the beggar in a pile of rags who is an angel. The instruction in each of these stories is to try to see the angel in the beggar.

"The incredible story the man told me reminded me of how all of us are walking in the valley of the shadow of death. Since I've had cancer, I'm particularly aware of [death] every day. How we walk in that valley determines everything. We all walk in the valley of the shadow of death, but the gift is to know it. If we know it, we can live our lives differently. When Jean Paul Sartre accepted a prize from the French government after World War II he said, 'We were never more free than when we were under the rule of Nazis.' He said, 'Everything we did, we did knowing we could die for it. Every word we spoke, we spoke knowing we could die for speaking it. We lived authentically.' That was also the teaching of this beggar. He appeared at a moment of prayer when I was open to a little miracle, so I could see what was being offered [to me]. That is awareness. If you move through the world with a willingness to see, the world in return moves toward you with a willingness to be seen. It's a dynamic of vision and revelation.

"I'm always looking for the story, always listening as a therapist might for the story, the ways events or images may be organizing themselves so we can see more deeply. For this reason, the process of teaching or working with a client is very exciting to me. As in writing a novel or poem, the images come together [when I am working with a client]. Also, I feel that the creative comes in the spirit of loving, that it really is a gift. When I'm teaching, I'm very moved. I have a sense of communication; something happens between people when they communicate with others."

Metzger travels the country teaching people how to write the story of their lives. "Telling our story possesses us unmercifully. Creating it and recreating it, our story becomes part of the way we construct ourselves. We must know our story because it is the source and record of our identity." Deena feels that it is difficult for some people to tell about grief, if grief is part of their story, because it is their own private information and by telling it they might discover their true identity. Often their story becomes a treadmill that can trap them, reducing them rather than informing and expanding. "By repeatedly telling a cover story, some people avoid the deeper, true story because they fear the unknown or because they have too much self-pity, self-righteousness or too much despair."

Metzger says that an authentic story is open-ended and can be transformed. Although it often gives us an impression that we have been there before, there is also something mysterious about it, something ambiguous. It must derive from something we know deeply and must be validated by our intelligence, intuition and heart. She quotes Isak Dinesen: "All suffering is bearable if it is seen as part of the story."

Since Metzger feels that the American culture promotes certain diseases, she explores healing in other cultures. "This is how healing is approached in the Navaho culture. A person who is ill is understood to be out of sync with nature, with animals, society, the culture and the gods. They understand illness as a serious imbalance or misalignment. Once the diagnosis is made, a singer finds the right chant that tells the myth of a hero who went through a similar situation. A likeness of the sick person and a particular moment that is relevant to him or her is drawn in the sand on the ground. Then chants are sung and the rituals are performed. Sometimes it takes days. During the ritual the whole community is gathered together and aligned with the person in the painting. In this way the gods are evoked. As the story is told, all the worlds are aligned. In the process of alignment, the illness is healed.

"So how did I live out that kind of healing since I'm not a Navaho?" Deena asks. "When my friends thought about me with deep love, I took that in as energy. Energy connects us in a way that makes us whole. We created a world in which such connections were real. We gathered together to support each other and created cultures that are opposed to the dominant culture."

Metzger calls the healing energy 'Tree,' which is also the name of her book. "'Tree' is the idea that we transmit energy to each other. When two or more individuals can really connect in one way or another, then they are made whole. Healing is created by making whole. That way we are integrated wholly in all the worlds." In her book *Tree*, she writes, "Love can be converted into beams of energy, which, when sent by one human being and received by another, can sustain, nurture, protect, heal and cure."

In addition to taking in the love of people who cared deeply for her, Metzger found out what was toxic in her life and transformed it. "For me it was feelings of unworthiness and overwhelming duty. Whenever I wanted to rest there were these voices, like the furies agitating me, haunting me. I could never rest, so I understood the voices to be toxic.

"But on a literal level, the foods we eat and the air we breathe is toxic. In order to live a healthy life I had to leave suburbia and move to a rural area. I live in a less formal and in a less gentrified way. Middle-class culture is toxic—consumerism, racism, ageism, gross materialism, violence and narcissism all lead to the breakdown of community and family. The major interest is in money, success and power," Metzger says.

Deena Metzger has been able to reach a remarkable sense of serenity and happiness as a result of the way she learned to live her life after the trauma of losing a part of her body. She offers a strong message of encouragement to others; she believes that healing requires living as authentic, as simply and a profound a life as possible. She says emphatically, "Whatever time you have, live it alive."

Alan Langer

"The world is full of 22-year-old men with surf boards who chew Wrigley's gum, or so our media images tell us," says Alan Langer. "You feel left out when you don't look like that. You feel isolated."

Langer, who has reddish-blond hair that recedes from a freckled brow, came down with multiple sclerosis (MS) when he was 32, almost 20 years ago. He sits in his Marblehead, Massachusetts home-office, on a three-wheeled electric scooter. From the neck down Langer is immobile, but his mind has an incomparable freedom. Life for him is full of loving and being loved, creative work and savoring the beauty of human connection.

Operating his computer with a mouth stick, Langer is working on his cable television series, *Ready, Willing, Enable.* Through the series, he is trying to reverse the feeling of isolation that many handicapped people feel and is providing a forum for services and activities.

"At the beginning," he says, from behind his telephone—a thin black wire that runs from ear to ear and curves out in front of his mouth—"several people are sitting on the set and they have labels on their foreheads—blind, black, elderly. Then they rip the labels off."

Langer has devoted himself to getting rid of the things that separate people. His position as a television producer uses his varied talents as an actor, a politician and a consultant.

"We're all tiny, frightened beings who are out on a huge ball whirling in space. All the lines and labels between us are artificial. From a distance you can't tell Kuwait from the other countries around it. Rand McNally drew the lines."

Like a photograph, Langer seems caught and frozen, but he emits a quiet light. The kinetic energy that MS has taken from his body seems to have converted to a concentrated mental energy that encompasses the people around him.

"Now I work hands-on, one-on-one, to help people who are disabled. I have an attitude toward disability. You are not your body. You have a value that exceeds what you can do. The idea for the TV series began from these thoughts. We are masters of our fate. Having MS has changed the direction of my life, but not its quality.

"If you've known life without a disability, when you become disabled, you feel life is not supposed to be that way. But this is the way life is.

"I have two choices: I can do the most with what I have or I can make myself unhappy because it didn't turn out the way I thought it ought to. When it rains out you can either enjoy it or curse it. My mother had an idea of what her life was supposed to be and if reality was different from what she wanted it to be, she made herself miserable. She only enjoyed three days out of the year. I never want to be like that.

"I see life like Monopoly. It really doesn't matter what piece you get to go around the board. When I was a kid we lost some of the pieces of our Monopoly game and so we substituted a screw and a bolt and, of course, it made no difference. What matters is how you play the game. The piece that I had broke in the middle of the game, but I haven't lost. In fact, I'm having more fun playing now than before.

"Consider Ruth Sienkiewicz Mercer, who has cerebral palsy and she can't move anything. Using a translator and a light board she wrote the book, *I Raise My Eyes to Say Yes*. Most people who are able-bodied haven't written a book. I haven't written a book. So who is to say who is disabled? What disables you is what's in your mind. Some people are remarkable. Think about the painter Christie Brown in the movie *My Left Foot* and the astrophysicist Stephen Hawking. Are they really disabled?

"There's always somebody worse off, so that I can look at where I am and feel fortunate. I know that however bad it gets there's always something I can do. It's how you hold the life you have. That's the difference between one person and another.

"There are some people whose whole lives are centered around being overweight. Then there are people who aren't even overweight, such as bulimics and anorexics, whose lives are still about being overweight. If you let circumstances affect you, it's your choice. Some people who are overweight are happy, so it can't only be the fact of being overweight that's causing these people to be unhappy."

Langer's symptoms began in 1973, oddly enough, soon after watching a TV program about people who were prime heart-attack candidates. The program upset him because his father died of a heart attack when Langer was 15 years old. He died with no warning; Langer just came home from school one day and found out that his father was dead.

"I was pretty disturbed by this television program and then the very next day, while I was in a meeting, my left hand began to tingle. During the meeting this feeling began to spread to my right hand and by the time we went out to lunch my legs had a strange feeling. They were stiff, and I had a hard time bending my knees.

"I went to a neurologist who had me feel some coins and say if they were nickels, dimes or quarters. He poked me with pins and asked me if the sensation was dull or sharp. Then he told me I was overly tense and that the feelings I was having were being caused by a case of bad nerves. I also went to a chiropractor. He said my problem was caused by hyperventilation.

"Around that time my brother and his wife came up for Passover. While we were having the Seder, I suddenly got very tired and I excused myself and went upstairs and lay down to take a short nap. I was suddenly awakened by a feeling that my face was swollen and that my eyes were swollen shut. I went into the bathroom and I looked in the mirror; I looked like the Werewolf of London. My face was distended and bloated. My nose was spread from one side of my face to the other and my eyes were little pig-like slits. I screamed and my brother and sister-in-law came up and they also screamed. My wife ran to a neighbor who was a doctor. He prescribed me some antihistamines. I took the pills and went to bed. By morning most of the swelling was gone.

"I continued to have this swelling once or twice a month for about a year. I went to an allergist who said I was allergic to walnuts. Everyone else seemed to feel that my symptoms were stress-related. I had a new job. I had just moved to Massachusetts and bought a new home and my marriage was on the verge of breaking up. I was a type A personality. Everything I did was a big production. I couldn't just buy a piece of real estate; I had to plan condos on it and turn it into a monumental business. I couldn't have a small idea. I needed to be a super achiever. I was also forceful and hard to be around. I came to the decision that the pressure I was putting on myself was the cause of the swelling. I decided that I was allergic to me.

"Whenever the symptoms would start, I would close my eyes and count backwards from ten and tried to relax. I practiced Transcendental Meditation (TM) and this would help the swelling to abate. At first it would take five or six hours, but after a few months I could stop the symptoms shortly after they would begin.

"In 1977 my condition got worse. By that time I had separated from my wife and was living by myself in Back Bay in Boston. When I walked I would stagger and I looked as if I were drunk. I went to the Lahey Clinic to see a neurologist. He did a spinal tap on me; it was negative for multiple sclerosis. I also went to a hypnotist who was able to provide me with some relief from the symptoms I was experiencing, but he wanted me to get an opinion from another neurologist, just to make sure there was no physical reason for my symptoms. So I went to a doctor at Beth Israel Hospital in Brookline, Massachusetts. He took a history and did some tests, one of which required that I draw a bicycle. On the basis of the results of the tests, he said he was 85 percent sure that I had MS. Right after delivering this information to me, he left the room to see another patient. Alone, I was absolutely devastated. I hadn't considered MS since I was told by the other neurologist that I didn't have it. At the time, I thought MS was like Lou Gehrig's disease and that it was terminal.

"By that time, I had remarried. My wife, Rachel, called the MS society and got some booklets. On the cover of one of the pamphlets there was a photograph of this guy who was sitting in a wheelchair and staring up at the sky. The article talked about how MS was 'the destroyer of young adults.' I was very put off by that. There was nothing positive in being destroyed. It was an attitude about a disease that I myself now had and I didn't want to have a negative picture like that about myself. My body felt brittle and weak and I no longer felt as if I was in control. My life was being destroyed by something unknown and unknowable.

"My wife and I had made plans to go to Nantucket that weekend, and even though I could barely walk, I went. I couldn't even lift the suitcases. Nothing interested me. My life felt like it was over. I used to feel that I could control my disease with my own mind, with meditation and with self-hypnosis. But, once the positive MS diagnosis was made, it made me feel that I couldn't control what was wrong with me and that there was nothing I could do to make anything better. Now neither TM nor hypnosis had a positive effect on me. My attitude was so negative. I had no control over what was destroying me. Maybe that was what caused the exaggeration of my symptoms during the time I was in Nantucket."

Langer began doing research and found out that MS was not terminal and that his symptoms could possibly level off. This information relaxed him somewhat. He also channeled his drive to perform into personal creativity.

In 1980 he left his job as a management consultant. He spent six months watching TV game shows and soap operas. He soon found that boring.

"Then, along with an associate, I founded a theater in Salem and did some acting. I had majored in acting in college. Then, after college, [I was diverted from acting when] I worked on Bobby Kennedy's campaign. Soon I was offered a political patronage job in the anti-poverty program. As I moved up the ladder, I got away from direct contact with people and more into administration and decisions on how to spend money. After getting MS I wanted to work directly with people again.

"The physical changes [I experienced] were so slow and gradual that I was able to adapt to them as they happened. It was like lifting a baby calf everyday. You don't notice that all of a sudden it has turned into a bull.

"I also became involved in a Unitarian Universalist church. One day when I was in church this woman I knew who also had MS sat behind me. I noticed that she was no longer using her cane. She leaned forward and asked me if I wanted to be cured. She told me about a woman named Peggy Huddleston who had studied at the Harvard Divinity School. I went to see Peggy who had a curing system that involved visualization and relaxation. She taught me how to get in touch with my higher self and how to move down to a level of consciousness where you are aware of all things and where you know the truth about yourself, a part of my consciousness that I call my 'pilot light.'

"From my higher self I learned that I created the MS so that I wouldn't die from a heart attack. I was blown away by that. I had been headed for a heart attack, which for me would have meant death, but the MS forced me to slow down.

"As my life's direction changed, so, in a way, did my personality. I began thinking more about other people than myself and was less obsessed by personal success. I came down with MS because I had a predisposition for it. Had I had a predisposition for being a diabetic I would have come down with that.

"In my work with Peggy, I visualized my spinal cord as a clean white sheath. I did that from that deep level of consciousness that she taught me to get down to. I began to understand that we create our own reality and that there's something about me that is part of everything and everyone.

"Soon I stopped walking with a cane and all my symptoms got better. I remember walking around in the kitchen and doing deep knee bends without having to hang onto anything. I didn't want to go to sleep because I feared my symptoms would return. When Peggy moved I stopped practicing the routine. I'm embarrassed now that I stopped."

In retrospect Langer wonders if on some deep level he felt that if his MS improved, it might have ended up causing the heart attack he thought he was destined to have had he not developed MS.

Langer coped with all the negative changes that occurred to his body by forcing himself to let go of many of the expectations he had had for himself, a task that his former wife had been unable to do. "My first wife didn't bargain for my MS. When we went out to eat, she would leave me at the door of the restaurant because I couldn't walk very far and then she resented having to park the car by herself. She had a lot of 'shoulds' about her life." The marriage to his first wife didn't last and he got remarried to a woman named Rachel.

"I knew from day one with Rachel that my limitations weren't important to her; they were not a problem. Her concerns were different. In 1982, when we first met, I was walking with a cane and by 1985, when we got married, I was using a wheelchair most of the time."

Together he and Rachel have turned negative situations into positive ones. When Langer did not receive the Electric Mobility Rascal that he had ordered, he called the New Jersey sales office and found out the salesman from whom he had ordered the Rascal had quit. When he and Rachel heard this, they drove to the office, and together they applied for and were offered the job. Rachel became a top traveling saleswoman and Alan made sales phone calls from home. Eventually, together they founded a company called Independence Unlimited, of which Langer is president. The company now has a multiple product line.

The Langers' home has 36-inch-wide accessible doorways through which Langer's scooter glides, and the Mobility Rascal allows him to stand in the kitchen when he and Rachel prepare Cajun, Oriental and Indonesian cuisine. "Cooking shared by two people is a special expression of love," says Langer.

They spend weekends driving in their van, hunting antiques. A barbershop pole stands in the corner of the living room which is decorated in American colors of red and blue. An antique iron, a variety of clay birds, pottery and other hand-hewn items decorate their house. They enjoy antiquing in Pennsylvania where they can also sample the Pennsylvania Dutch food.

"I think we both wish we could get dressed up, me in a tuxedo and Rachel in an evening dress, and walk into a place and dance. I wish I could hold the chair out for her. I also miss building things around the house, gardening, feeling my hands in the dirt, pulling out the weeds and touching the flowers. And I wish I could help Rachel more.

"But I don't let these wishes get in the way of enjoying what we do have. If you have one picture in your mind, there's no room for another picture and you can be diminished by it.

"Luckily, there are lots of things I like to do and for

the things I can no longer do, I've substituted other things. Having other options removed has freed me up to do the TV series which is a labor of love.

"Last November we drove down to the Epcot Center in Florida. We did the trip in 300-mile bites and stopped along the way in Alexandria, Virginia and Savannah, Georgia to sightsee. When problems came up, like not having wheelchair access, we found a way to deal with them. Rachel's attitude is like mine. She's flexible and deals with my physical problems as an inconvenience, as a condition of life, rather than something tragic.

"What is me is beyond my physical body. I'm not a religious person like Mother Teresa, and I'm anything but selfless. My spiritual side doesn't grow out of any training, but from a knowledge deeper than belief. Certain things touch that piece of knowing. Real doctors know there's a component to healing that's beyond medical science that's in the patient."

Langer tries consciously to develop a sixth sense which he views as a mysterious antenna or invisible wire connecting him to powers beyond himself. "It's the same part of the person where great creativity is. People like Mozart can tap into their pilot light. They can break through the barriers that protect it and when it's opened they create great art. I'm not talking about being famous; that may take something else. I'm talking about the ability to move other people. Call it love, vulnerability, sensitivity, openness, acceptance. It's tapping an energy source that exists out there. They have to work on their instrument—their paints and their brushes, but more than that they have to touch the source at will, to contact different levels of their being.

"Different inventions are worked on by different peo-ple in different parts of the world. The automobile was being worked on at the same time by Italians and Ameri-cans who had no contact with each other. Illnesses are cured in different parts of the world at the same time by people open to a certain level of creativity. These things existed out there. It's a matter of hooking into them, of somehow holding your wire out and getting the messages, wherever they come from.

"We are where we are supposed to be given our experiences. If we weren't where we were supposed to be the whole world would explode. The kind of order we find in our universe can't be accidental. Think of it. Two cells get together and nine months later there's a human being. Science fiction isn't even that bizarre.

"Expectations cause us heart ache. At 31 I had a picture in my mind of what my marriage was going to look like, what the kids were going to look like. Expectations lead to disappointment. If someone had told me then that I would get MS I would have been angry.

"I was an achievement person. I was always climbing up the ladder. I was a type A personality and the MS forced me to slow down. I was able to indulge my fantasies. I started a theater and it was wonderful. I found things that needed my expertise as a consultant and my love of acting. If I didn't get the MS I wouldn't have been able to do all the things I've done.

"I'm a paraplegic, but my life is fantastic. I'm doing the kinds of things I was born to do."

Eleanor and Dick Grace

When she was 16, Doreen Grace wrote a poem to her mother in which she asks: "Who is it that I am? I have resigned myself to the fact that the answers shall elude me throughout my earthly existence.... I am frustrated and reduced to a state of confusion."

Ironically, Doreen did not know at that time that her earthly existence would only last another five years. Then, she was a gifted college student, preparing for a promising future, but soon she would contract a fatal virus that would destroy much of her brain. The confusion expressed in her poem is an uncanny premonition; because of the damage to her brain, she lived her last two years as a radically different person than what she had been. Her judgment became so impaired, in fact, that she once drank cleaning fluid, and left teeth marks on the soap in the bathroom. Her intelligence and thoughtfulness survived in her poems and other writings, but tragically, Doreen could eventually no longer read. After the brain damage occurred, for 15 months until she died, the Graces cared diligently for Doreen, but they felt isolated from medical information and from other families who were going through the same thing. On the day of her death, her parents decided to devote the rest of their lives to fighting diseases of the brain and to helping others who have a family member plagued with neurological disorders. In response, Dick and Eleanor Grace founded and built The Doreen Grace Brain Center, a clearinghouse of information on brain diseases.

The Center is in a most unlikely spot: on the southern side of Cape Cod, on New Seabury's peninsula, off the brilliant blue waters of the Nantucket Sound.

Following a winding road, one weaves past private villas offset from the street by small forests and a championship golf course. The Doreen Grace Brain Center is located on Promontory Point on the southern side of Cape Cod. The road curves and at its end point, the magnificent structure, surrounded by dune grass and shrubs, is revealed. Three stories of glass and gray clapboard siding, it is designed to symbolize the two sides of the brain.

The Doreen Grace Brain Center provides a serene and relaxed atmosphere where neuroscience professionals mingle with families of those with stroke, epilepsy, brain tumors, encephalitis, Alzheimer's and Parkinson's disease, multiple sclerosis, Huntington's chorea and other neurological disorders.

Inside, Dick and Eleanor Grace, both tall and silver-haired, graciously give me a tour of the Center. High ceilings, soft gray colors and skylights give every room a feeling of spaciousness. Meeting places range in size from intimate alcoves to the large amphitheater that has an enclosed balcony that seats almost 150 people. Luminous stained-glass windows offer artistic interpretations of the left and right side of the brain. The paintings, carving and sculpture of 28 different artists are everywhere. Several of Doreen's poems are framed along the walls of the elegant building. The Graces have made this endeavor a tribute to their daughter's life as well as an attempt to keep others from suffering death due to the same disease and related disorders.

A stunning part of the Graces' accomplishment is that almost everything—the land, the sheetrock, the cement, the electrical and telephone systems, nails, wood, paint, shades, artwork and even much of the labor needed to built the gigantic and ornate construction— was donated. In 1977, the Graces, who, at that time owned a small advertising agency, began to raise funds for the building of the Brain Center by running hot air balloon races from Barnstable County Fairgrounds to Provincetown, but the majority of the donations came from business people and civic organizations to whom the Graces had told the story of their daughter's life and death. As if moved by some larger force, people appeared with exactly what was needed at the right time. Every single one of those who helped were strangers — none of them wanted any recognition for their magnanimous donations of time, energy, money—and more impor- tantly, the care they felt for others. Several of Doreen's poems are framed along the walls of the elegant building. The Center is a tribute to Doreen Grace's life. As well, it is an attempt to help others who are in the same situation.

Eleanor and Dick sit at the long table in the richly paneled conference room and describe the ordeal that inspired the building, research, conference and educational center. Eleanor does most of the talking, but now and then Dick cuts in to clarify a point.

Eleanor says, "It was Christmas vacation of her sophomore year in 1974, and on that day Doreen was getting ready to be a bridesmaid at the wedding of her best friend. She started to have flu-like symptoms, but didn't have a fever. She complained of a terrible headache and walked through the house screaming, 'My God, my God, I can't stand it.' I called a neighbor, Mary, who was a doctor. She came over and one of the questions she asked Doreen was, 'Do you know who I am?' It took Doreen a few minutes to answer and that was frightening, but then I figured she was confused because her head hurt. Mary said there wasn't much we could do since we didn't know what was going on, but if her temperature rose, we should take her to the hospital at once.

"Our son Richard came home from a hockey game

and he was upstairs with Doreen. 'Come quick, come quick,' he said, 'Doreen is talking kooky.' So I went up and Doreen was really upset. She was saying, 'And what's so funny about going to Mass in a hockey rink?' I said, 'Well, Doreen, you have Mass in church and hockey in a hockey rink.' She said, 'Something's happening to my brain. I think I have a brain tumor.' I said, 'You read too much. Let's not talk about brain tumors.' She said, 'Mom, I know something's happening. I can't control what I'm thinking.'

"We got through dinner and then about 3 in the morning Doreen woke up. She put on all the lights, scattered her school books and papers all over the place and was staring at an *Architectural Digest*, but not reading it. She left a tea kettle on the stove whistling loudly and got up and went to the bathroom. She had a hairbrush in her hand and was staring with huge glassy eyes into the mirror and saying, 'I'm trying, I'm trying.' I asked her what she was trying and she didn't answer me so I turned her around. I'd never seen anyone with eyes so glossed, but I'd never seen anyone going into a coma before. I said, 'Who am I?'

"She said, I don't know. I've never seen you before in my life.'"

Eleanor clamps her hand to her throat and lets out a long-winded sigh. "I will never forget that scene as long as I live. Then I saw this vomit on her bed. I'd never seen so much vomit in all my life and later I thought it looked just like little brains all over her room.

"My heart was pounding when I took her temperature. It was 103.5. So we got her all washed and dressed and drove 90 miles an hour to the hospital. I had to sit on her in the car because she was out of control. She ate the lapel off her jacket and started to chew on the rings on her fingers. When we got to the emergency room, I had to tell them not to put the thermometer in her mouth or she'd eat it.

"I heard someone say, 'She's dying.' And I thought, 'Oh, my God. They can't be saying what they are saying.'

They put on masks because they didn't know what Doreen had. They thought it might be something contagious. They asked if she ate any exotic food or was around any strange animals. Then they told us to get a priest because Doreen was dying. Then Doreen became violent and ripped all the tubes out, so they had to restrain her.

"At 9:30 that night they said we could go home and take a break and no sooner had we got in the house that they called and said to come back. Doreen had been diagnosed with acute herpes simplex encephalitis. The staff at the hospital wanted to know what parts of Doreen's body we wanted to donate. People thought I was in shock and I guess I was in shock, but I said very clearly 'Her eyes.' I thought it was a shame that people die and don't donate [their body parts] to help others.

"I was numb. We all held hands and prayed. I said, 'My God, please give us the strength to face what's ahead.' I didn't ask God not to let Doreen die. I didn't ask for a miracle. On the way back to the hospital I called a priest, Father Frank, and I told him about Doreen. She had been at a stage in her life when she didn't know if she wanted to be in the Catholic faith. She did a lot of reading about other religions and talked to a lot of priests and theologians. One week before she got sick she went to St. Patrick's Cathedral in New York and received communion. So when Father Frank came, he pointed to Doreen's coat and said, 'That's your daughter's coat.' I asked him how he knew that. He said he saw Doreen come up the aisle on Christmas Eve. She had been one of the last ones to receive holy communion and he was so impressed with her because she looked like the Madonna.

"He gave Doreen the rights of the living. We went on like that [while Doreen was in a coma] for days and weeks. We watched Doreen waste away day after day. Her hair fell out, her prettiness went. She got worse and worse and they said if she survived she would be a complete vegetable. I had these feelings when I wanted to pull all the tubes out and put myself in her bed. It was so awful to see her waste away. The doctors and nurses gave up on her. They kept saying she was going to die and prepared us for her death six times. Somehow people got word and prayer groups started praying for her.

"Then, one morning, after Doreen had been in the coma for 45 days, I went to the hospital and they said they had something they wanted to tell me. They said Doreen was going to come out of the coma. I laughed and I said, 'I know. I don't know what is going to happen, but I know she's coming out.'

"One night I was in the hospital reading the Bible. I had tears in my eyes and felt them coming down my cheek and I was actually talking to God. I said, how could I have lived so many years and not have seen so many things that were so simple. So many things about what life was about. This man in a dark blue suit was there, and he put his hand on my shoulder and said he had admired us and prayed for us and had been devastated by what was happening. He was a minister from California and his mother had just died. When I talked to him, I just flowed and he said I was full of the holy spirit and that he knew I had a strength in me. He also said that Doreen was going to be his inspiration for his next sermon when he returned to California.

"After that meeting I knew that the physical part of Doreen, the part that had wasted away, was not what was important. What was important was her spirituality. We knew about that from her battle to know God and to study every religion. She was such a beautiful person and we would work as hard as we could so that she might go back to society."

After many, many weeks in a coma, Doreen started to wake up. "She was almost bald, her face shrunk from all the weight she lost. Her nostrils were raw. One day she was sitting in front of a mirror and looking at herself and then she stuck her tongue out at herself. I would go in every day and say things like, 'I wore your sweater today. Are you going to be mad at me for stretching it out?' Nothing. Her eyes were opened and looked. I pulled her head up and she just stared at me. I didn't know if she knew who I was or not.

"I went to Mass the next day and asked God for direction. I built up a strength and a fight inside me. I asked God that I might again see her walk, see her talk and that she would know me. I said, 'God, I don't know what the plan is, but I have to ask one favor. May she know us? Please, could she say, 'Hi Mom, hi Dad, hi Richard?'" As Eleanor recounts this memory she says, "This brings me to tears."

"Doreen went from the hospital to a rehabilitation center. When we went to visit her there, I saw her all slumped over in a chair. I said to Dick, 'I don't know if I can handle this' and he said, 'Yes you can.' I heard one of the staff say, 'This is the patient with brain damage.' That was the first time I had heard those two words and it blew my mind, more than when they said Doreen was going to die. I thought, 'Oh my God, they are really saying she is severely brain damaged. And she had such a wonderful brain.'

"We really battled back. Dick and I used to take her out in a wheelchair. Everyone else had given up. We were opened up to a whole new world and were exposed to all these people who didn't have anybody to love them. There was this lonely black woman who we'd give a hug and we finally got her to smile. She was just one of many people who sat day after day with no one visiting them. It seemed so sad.

"Pretty soon Doreen was walking and I started to show her how to chew her food. A man who was in his sixties and had seen Doreen every day said that Doreen talked, and I wondered why she wasn't talking to us. It was because people talked down to her and treated her like she was a baby. This man said that she picks up the elderly people's feet and puts them back on their wheelchair when they fall off and helps people eat, but never when someone in a white uniform was in the room. She must have been angry. I lifted her head and said, 'Doreen, that's your name. Do you know who I am?' She just stared and finally she whispered, 'cleaning woman.' I said, 'Yes, I've been your cleaning woman for all those years. I'm your mother.'

"She put her hands on my face and said, 'How could I forget someone as beautiful as my mother. I'll never forget you again.' I went running out to get the doctors, but when I came back, she didn't know who I was. It was so sad to have my hopes destroyed. That night I totally accepted the brain damage. The next day [the staff at the rehabilitation center] said, 'We are having a party for the brain damaged' and I said we'd be there. Doreen was starting to grow hair and someone had bought her a beautiful pair of earrings. She looked so cute. When they turned her around in the chair, she said, 'Hi Mom, hi Dad, hi Richard,' and I got down on my knees in front of the whole place and said, 'God, thank you. Now I know whatever happens, I can handle it.'

"Kathy, Doreen's friend who was getting married, never went on a honeymoon. She came to intensive care every day and stayed until midnight. Later, when Doreen was in rehabilitation, she and her husband flew down from Canada to see Doreen and Kathy was so emotional she couldn't talk at all. Doreen looked out the window at the parking lot and said, 'It's so gross.' She meant there weren't any trees. Then she turned to Kathy and said, 'You realize I can no longer communicate with you.' She knew what was happening to her.

"We had to think about where Doreen would go when she left the rehabilitation center. The [staff] said she should be put away, warehoused in an institution, because [they thought] we couldn't handle her, but we said no. I couldn't believe the world was so cold. We contacted Northeastern University's speech and hearing clinic in Boston and found two students, both Doreen's age, who could be teachers and companions for her."

After 15 months, on March 5, 1976, Doreen died of a seizure caused by the herpes simplex virus that had destroyed most of her brain. "To lose a child—at least the way Doreen had lived and died—was like going to the pits of hell. The night Doreen died my whole life passed before me and I thanked God for my wonderful husband and for the 21 years we'd had with Doreen. On January 31, she turned 21. I remember running down the street and saying, 'Our daughter died.' I vacuumed the rugs all night and I heard Dick get up and I heard him cry. He had found one of these square pieces of wood we'd been teaching her to count with and it was the number 21; he left it on the window sill. Doreen had been unable to tell us how old she was. It was as if she left the number to tell us she finally could tell her age.

"After the funeral, I cleaned out her bedroom and threw all her belongings on her bed—her birth certificate, awards, death certificate. She was so young. She had no life. Most of her life was written in her poetry.

"I didn't know where I would go from there. So much had happened, it was like it hadn't happened. We had to take it just one day at a time. We had been such private people.

"I read all of Doreen's psychology and philosophy books and what she had underlined. I knew Dick was waiting for me to come back to the world, but I didn't want to. Richard had his first job and I'd pick him up for lunch and we'd go down to the dock at Falmouth on Cape Cod. I couldn't go to the beach where Doreen used to write her poetry. Friends used to call me up to play tennis, but I didn't want to. I had a terrible summer. Then we got called on to do a seminar on death and dying." Eleanor realized that, if nothing else, they could at least be of help to others. "We were introduced to a young woman, Paula, who had leukemia and our emotions were very touched. What do you say to someone who is 21 and dying? Paula was worried that her parents wouldn't let her say that she was dying. She said she knew she was going to die. People know these things.

"When we did the seminar, Dick and I went on the college stage and had four hours of tough questioning from an audience of hundreds. 'Do you hate God? How have you changed?' I answered that we don't go to parties anymore or social activities that are unrelated to helping others. We do things with a purpose and have devoted the rest of our lives to brain research. The night Doreen died we donated her brain. We talked to several doctors and said we really wanted to do something and felt frustrated. We wanted to have a place where we could funnel information and support basic brain research and which would help us overcome all the central nervous system diseases. How could we bring medical people together so they could exchange ideas? That's how the concept of the Brain Center came about.

"We started with $42 of Doreen's savings. The first year we went around New England doing presentations and just making people aware. Our first fundraiser was a hot air balloon race, followed by other balloon races.

"We went to Washington and did a presentation before the World Neuroscience Board and they gave us 15 minutes to speak. Afterward, we got a standing ovation. We needed medical backing and it was mind-boggling to have those top brains from the whole country be so supportive.

"Then we had to be serious about creating the Brain Center. Chris Burden, president of New Seabury on Cape Cod, said we should come down and choose some land. That started the project. It took several more years to get enough money to start the actual construction. Dick had been a Marine, and he went to them and told them about our plans for the Brain Center. They cleared the land and helped us put up the structure. There was this wonderful stepping forth of people and it brought our faith in humanity back.

Dick, who had listened to Eleanor thoughtfully as she spoke, added that Doreen's illness and death had changed him. "People make promises when they are trying to get out of a situation, but when I got back from serving in the Marines, I forgot the earlier promise I had made to God in combat. I got involved in getting ahead and when this happened to Doreen, I felt that God said to me, 'I called in your chips. The things you told me, you didn't do.' Now I realize that the things that were once so big are, in actuality, so small. Things like houses, cars and vacations. Now I like to express my feelings through artwork. I realized that Doreen's story had to be shared with others. It changed our lives and we learned a lot that we can pass on.

"The people who helped were total strangers to us. None of them wanted any recognition. Doreen seemed to put the team together. Everything we needed just seemed to arrive.

"One of the donators was this young man who had once fallen down an elevator shaft. His head could have been severely damaged, but all he suffered was a gash in his thigh. When he got up, he promised God that he'd never forget it, but then he bought a house and a car and had kids and did forget. Meeting us made him remember. I believe God puts people in your path through your life's journey. Some of us recognize that we should be interacting and some of us don't. People come into our lives for a purpose." Dick and Eleanor Grace realized their own purpose through their daughter's illness and death. Eleanor sums it up:

"Never once did we say, 'Why us?' Never did I feel angry at God. To have lived and to have never known Doreen would have been [more of a] tragedy."

Armando Valladares

Armando Valladares spent 22 years as a political prisoner in Cuba. Almost daily he was savagely beaten and doused with buckets of urine and excrement. He was denied medical attention for the fractured bones in his leg and, worse, he was the victim of medical experiments designed to investigate scurvy, edema and pellagra, which left him partially paralyzed.

Valladares mentally escaped the torture by writing poetry—his way of "challenging the terrible reality that pressured me and beat me up. Poetry was like a rebel yell that let my spirit free to go outside."

As soon as the guards discovered that Valladares was writing, they took his pen and paper away, but this did not stop him; he continued to write on toilet paper and used his own blood for ink. "I created suns that could not be extinguished, horizons which could not be barbed-wired."

A book of his poems, *From My Wheelchair*, was eventually published and translated into several different languages. Valladares became known worldwide and French president François Mitterrand intervened to help him gain freedom, which Castro finally granted in 1982. In 1987, President Ronald Reagan appointed Valladares ambassador to the U.S. Human Rights Commission to the United Nations.

In 1960, when Valladares was 23, he awakened to the cold steel of a machine gun muzzle that was being pushed against his temple. Four armed men from Castro's Political Police came to the house where Valladares lived with his mother and his sister to arrest him. They searched the house very thoroughly, flipping through books, page by page, and opening jars and bottles, but they could not find any "evidence" to use against him.

At the time, Valladares worked in a postal savings bank (which had become attached to the Ministry of Communication during the Revolution), and he had occasionally voiced a negative attitude about communism. He also refused to place a pro-Castro slogan on his desk that read, "If Fidel is a Communist, then put me on the list. He's got the right idea." He naively thought that the worst his employers would do as a result of his attitude would be to fire him, just as they had done to one of his friends.

But he was very mistaken. Valladares was fingerprinted and photographed with a sign in front of him that read "COUNTERREVOLUTIONARY." He was told that because he had studied in a school that was run by priests who were known as counterrevolutionaries, by association he, too, was a counterrevolutionary. Valladares responded that Castro also had studied in a school taught by Jesuits. Valladares, stunned by the entire situation, told them that they had no evidence that he was a "counterrevolutionary." But the guards paid no attention: "We have the conviction that you are a potential enemy of the Revolution. For us, that is enough."

Valladares was then locked in a room with other prisoners—people he'd never seen before—and they were then photographed and filmed. These photographs were printed in the newspaper, which reported that the men were terrorists, CIA agents, who were now Castro's prisoners. Valladares was then taken to the La Cabana prison, a castle-like, medieval fortress. Executions by firing squads were performed nightly in its surrounding dry, deep moats.

Valladares listened to his fellow prisoners yell "Long Live Christ the King!" just before they were shot. The cries became a potent symbol of the prisoners' bravery, integrity and rebellion. At first, Valladares realized that Christ was there for him in the moments when he prayed that he would not be killed, but that seemed to be a utilitarian kind of religion. Later, he realized that Christ gave life (and death, if it came to that) ethical meaning.

"Christianity became more than a religious faith. It became a way of life for me. Because of my situation, it seemed my life would necessarily be a life of resistance, but I would be sustained in it by a soul filled with love and hope."

During his trial, the president of the tribunal crossed his feet on the table, leaned back in his chair and read a comic book; he had no need to pay attention since Valladares' sentence had been decided beforehand; although there was not one piece of evidence against him, he was found guilty of public destruction. Valladares was appalled that the officials had no need for any concrete evidence of his alleged destruction of public property— such as the name of the building he was supposed to have damaged. He compared his situation to convicting a person of murder without ever producing a corpse and without the accused, not to mention the accusers, even knowing who he was supposed to have killed.

Following his conviction, Valladares was sent to the largest Cuban prison which was located offshore, on the Isla de Pinos. Built in 1939, the prison was shaped like an enormous beehive. It was there that Valladares learned the art of mental control. For example, to survive he had to eat, and in order to eat he had to get over being squeamish about eating the yellow-white worms that infested all the food they were given to eat. He would tell himself, "They are harmless; they have been boiled in the steam vats and in China, people eat insects."

Another important aspect of Valladares' ability to stay alive was establishing solidarity with the other inmates. They worked together to gather news of the outside world and this helped keep prison life in perspective. One of the inmates constructed a rudimentary radio which allowed them to hear the news. Then six copies, one for the inmates housed on each floor, were transcribed and the news was read in small groups. In order to communicate with each other without being heard, the prisoners invented a special sign language and they also used Morse code. A nylon fishing line was rigged up so that they could slide letters across the prison yard to the inmates who were too far away to see hand signals. This communication line was eventually discovered by a guard when a bird perched on it.

After the failed Bay of Pigs invasion in April 1961, the guards became even more ruthless and violent. They buried boxes of TNT under the prison yard and also stashed it in the watchtowers; the prisoners were told they would be blown up if there was another invasion attempt. Some of the prisoners were explosives experts and were able to figure out a way to deactivate the central fuse. They cut through the hose that connected all the fuses and replaced the two inches that was filled with TNT with an empty cylinder. They then sewed it back together. The fuse was like a garden hose and the government technicians frequently yanked on it to make sure that it hadn't been cut. Because the prisoners had sewn it back together, the guards were not able to tell that the prisoners had deactivated the entire system.

The government decided to set up a program of "rehabilitation" where freedom was promised to the prisoners if they complied with various requests that included, among other things, revealing secret information about other "counterevolutionaries" and submitting a written apology for their counterrevolutionary activities. Valladares wanted and had no part of this.

With three other friends, he spent much of his time planning an escape. The prisoners dyed material and sewed uniforms that looked just like the soldiers'. On the night of the escape, with a hacksaw blade they cut through their cells' iron bars, then rubbed their bodies with kerosene to hide their scent from the dogs they knew the officials would soon send after them once they discovered their escape. When Valladares jumped from his second-floor cell, he fractured and dislocated bones in his foot, but managed to walk without limping as he moved past the guards who assumed he was one of them.

Pouring pepper in their footsteps to cover their scent, they made their way to the mouth of the Jucaro River where a boat and crew was supposed to be waiting to pick them up and take them away. They waited for the boat for several days, but it never arrived. Eventually they were found by a prison search party.

The director of the prison took the escape as a personal affront; Valladares and the other recaptured prisoners became the objects of his sadistic reaction. They were locked in "punishment cells" and the doors were welded shut. One of the guards jumped on Valladares' leg which was already fractured in three places. When Valladares asked for medical attention for his badly swollen and blue leg, a guard replied that he hoped he'd get gangrene so they could cut his leg off. Valladares and his colleagues were slopped with pails of urine and excrement, poked at with a pole whenever they tried to sleep and were denied eating utensils for the cold food they were given. Since they didn't want to eat with excrement-covered hands, they ate like animals, grabbing the food from the bowls with their mouths.

"What saved me from animality," Valladares explains, "was inventing interior worlds. I filled them with light, air, flowers and stars and pleasant sounds—bird songs, waves on the shore, branches swishing against trees. I just closed my eyes and found a light within me that was out of the guard's grasp. In my mind I could wander across meadows and live in a secret world where I was free." He asked God for the strength to bear up under the conditions without being consumed with hatred. His spirituality became his shield.

After a while, Valladares was transferred to another "punishment ward." Fortunately, the ward was headed by a prisoner who was also a doctor. The doctor ordered that Valladares be bathed and that his leg, which now was covered with a horrible fungus, be attended to. The fungus was peeled off his leg like the rind of a fruit. The doctor took x-rays of his foot but there wasn't much they could do. It had been neglected for so long that it had knitted together badly and his toes had turned inward.

Rebelling against having to stay so long in the punishment ward, Valladares and his fellow escapees went on a hunger strike and when the prisoners from other wards joined in support, the officials finally let them return to their regular cells. Valladares was starting to realize that for him pain was becoming the force that motivated him not to give up and to continue to struggle.

After spending so many years in solitary confinement, Valladares knew the importance of human contact. He set up a social club in which he and the other prisoners made a carpet and crude teacups, and they sat yoga-style while one of them read aloud from books that had been smuggled in by various relatives. They sat beneath a cover emblazoned with the hammer-and-sickle symbol and read anything from Chinese philosophy to adventure stories. In this way they were able to create an oasis in the midst of the cruel and subhuman prison environment.

Secretly, Valladares and the other prisoners built a little Christmas tree out of a broom and wire. They hung cotton balls, egg shells and medicine bottles on it for decoration. Although Castro had abolished the observance of Christmas, the prisoners were able to find a way to celebrate it, and they didn't let their horrible surroundings prevent them from doing so.

Sharing activities and lending support to his fellow prisoners helped him feel more like a valid human being. Companionship was important to him because nine of the 22 years he was imprisoned were spent in solitary, minuscule cells. As he told the 44th session of the UN Commission on Human Rights, he had spent "eight thousand days struggling to show that I was still a human being...and struggling not to allow the hatred that my atheist guards sought to sow with their bayonets to flower in my heart."

When confronted by the guards' sadistic behavior, Valladares told himself that perhaps they acted with such hatred and vengeance toward him because they had heard stories that were not true, that he had bombed buildings and maybe even hurt innocent people. But their brutality seemed to come from a place that he could not comprehend; they seemed to have virtually no understanding and compassion for other human beings.

In his talks to the United Nations, Valladares shared the story of his friend, Fernando Lopez del Toros, who began to feel that his life of sacrifice was useless and took his own life by cutting his jugular vein. "Fernando was the victim of indifference, of silence, of that terrible echoless universe in which in this century of horrors and violations so many good men and women die. The persecuted must know that people of good will are with them."

To that end, when Valladares was released, he went to Madrid where he founded the European Coalition for Human Rights in Cuba. Like Amnesty International, the organization works for the human dignity of all political prisoners.

"We have to reach into the cells of all the world's Fernando Lopez del Toros to tell them with firmness and solidarity, in some corner, in your honor and in your memory, there will always be the note of a violin, the voice of compassion of those who will defend you. Look, you are not an animal. Do not take your life. Liberty will never disappear from the face of the earth.

"At times when one is treated like a beast, the only thing that saves you is knowing that somewhere, someone loves you, respects you, fights to return you to your dignity."

For the prisoners that he left behind in Cuba, Valladares has become that someone.

Victor Davidoff

Victor Davidoff, a former political prisoner, feels like he's living in two different worlds. "Our main office is on Wall Street, and you can imagine the environment with the computers, the reports, the money counting up to millions of dollars. That's what I do from 9:00 to 5:00. I pick up the *New York Times*, I go to the deli to get lunch. Then I have these lapses. Strange feelings, recollections, recalls. I don't know how to say it in English. For moments, I am again in the Special Psychiatric Hospital and can see the color of the walls and the Siberian winter outside." It is clear that while Davidoff has moved in a positive direction since the torment he suffered as a political prisoner, he is still very much in the process of healing.

When he was a third-year law student, Davidoff wrote a book about the Soviet legal system during the reign of Joseph Stalin. When one of Davidoff's friends was arrested and his apartment searched, Soviet authorities found Davidoff's manuscript and other works he had written. Davidoff was charged with "slandering the Soviet system" and found to have "sluggish schizophrenia," a diagnosis that was frequently given to dissenters. The official document said that "Davidoff suffers from emotional, volitional disorders, a decline of his critical faculties...." According to Soviet theory, sluggish schizophrenia is a progressive condition with minimal chances for improvement. The symptoms are "grandiose

191

ideas of reforming the world or offering new inventions of outstanding significance."

The diagnosis made it possible for the KGB to deprive him of his civil rights and to send him, not to a camp for a definite term, but to a mental institution for an indefinite term. Once he was diagnosed as mentally ill, even his father, the dean of a law school, could not help him get out.

During the time he was in the psychiatric hospital, Davidoff could not control his actions or his thoughts. Even his mind—the last resource a prisoner has—was violated, invaded by hallucinations from the powerful drugs that he was forced to take. When he looked at a wall, he thought only about a wall; in other words, his thinking process was dead. When he tried to talk, he forgot the first part of the sentence before he could get to the end of it. The drugs made him restless, so he paced his cramped cell—three steps forward and three steps back—and he did this all day long. Sometimes Davidoff believed that he was in a desert and felt that his mouth and lungs were filled with dry, hot sand. Other times, he thought he saw animals and believed he was going insane and because he had little control over his actions, he was terrified that he might attack someone. If this had happened, the guards would have tied Davidoff down and repeatedly given him medications that were so powerful they could have killed him.

Davidoff's memories split off from his consciousness and took on a life of their own. Now, he says, when he comes home from work and looks in his refrigerator, for instance, he has flashbacks. The gray odor of boiled cabbage from the prison seems to fill the air, and he suddenly feels as if he is still sitting in a small cell, wearing rags, his head shaved, trying to slurp up a bowl of cabbage soup.

Although it has been 11 years since Davidoff was originally confined, he has never been able to escape the clammy terror of the prison walls. Aftershocks of the three years and eight months of chemical torture that he endured have made rebuilding his life difficult. Although he has physical scars—a puffy hand that was frostbitten after he was forced to squat in the snow for several hours and a fractured right eye socket from a beating—the psychological scars are much worse. These include short-term memory loss, sleeplessness, nightmares, depression, difficulty trusting people, trouble concentrating, exaggerated startle responses, constricted emotions, and feelings of detachment and estrangement from others.

Davidoff found help with the flashbacks and other symptoms of posttraumatic stress at the Center for the Rehabilitation of Torture Victims in Roseland, New Jersey. For 18 months Davidoff worked with a social worker, Doug Gerber, and dredged up the rage and humiliation that he had suppressed. Expressing these emotions while he was in prison would have put his life in jeopardy.

His recovery process is not yet complete, but now he's working on his own. As a form of therapy he's writing a book about his incarceration. He is also on the board of directors of the Center for the Rehabilitation of Torture Victims so that he can help others.

But Davidoff's trauma, which in psychological terms has not been "fully integrated," continues to fragment and control his life. "I have two lives," he says. "The second life is only three or four years old. All the main feelings I had—hopes, feelings, joy, happiness, frustration, distress—happened in the first life. If I forget about my first life, I start to feel like I am 15 years old again, uncertain and unsure."

Gray streaks in his brown hair and beard and a deadpan way of speaking make him seem older than he is. He is only 36 years old. His face looks fuller now than a picture that was taken of him in 1983 in the Kuibyshev Psychiatric Hospital, but thick, round spectacles still give him a look of meekness.

His words are slightly nuanced by Russian pronunciation and sometimes he apologizes for being unable to say what he means in English. Frequently, he brushes his beard or twists a hank of hair around a forefinger as he sips his beer.

"Now I still get into some troubles, but if I compare them to the troubles of my first life, they're a joke, not a trouble. When I watch movies and see these people trying to kill each other and trying to make ten million dollars, I think, 'What is that all about? They don't have troubles at all.'

"Also, I remain in two different dimensions. Life in prison and life on the outside are totally different. In prison, I wanted peace—a situation where nobody would bother me, frighten me, or give me pain or drugs. I wanted them to leave me alone. In this life I have to be active. I have to be industrious. I have to be aggressive sometimes, for example, when I was looking for a job.

"There are different values in the United States. They are not limited to just reaching a minimum level. For example, I had a used car and I decided to get a better car and lose more money. It took a great deal of time to find a reasonable car. I had to go around and talk to these many auto dealers. But this would have been absurd from my point of view in 1983. Then, I wanted the minimum to survive and did not want to want more."

In the United States, Davidoff studied computer science at Long Island University. He prefers talking to computers rather than to people. "I suffer a lot because in Russian I had a good style, with poetry. It is very painful for me to know I am not proficient in the language I speak."

Davidoff also finds it difficult to write freely, since in Russia he always had to worry about the censor. "I use more conventional phrases, instead of something uncommon. This is the feeling of someone in a psychiatric prison who has to prove each day that he is not insane. When I do something I think, 'Is it normal or can it be considered to be abnormal?' I have a bad habit of talking to myself which I developed when I was in solitary cells in 1980. And whenever I talk to myself I worry that someone will think that I am crazy."

Talking to machines also makes Davidoff feel safer because in prison it was dangerous to talk with other people. When speaking to the nurses or doctors, he had to watch every word he spoke.

The orderlies who were in charge of him were also criminals and some of his fellow inmates were criminally insane. One prisoner had shot five people including three children and another had raped and killed his own sister. "One of my cellmates, my friend for two years, he was kept there until the last year [of his sentence] and, within three months of his release, he died of cancer. I can't forget about it, and I feel it all the time. Not every moment, but somewhere it's kept." Davidoff recalls that the nurses seemed to enjoy subjecting the prisoners to suffering, and the psychiatrists, who wore the green uniform of prison wardens under their white smocks, "would not hesitate to kill for a single word of contradiction or a word spoken at the wrong time."

"I was at the bottom of the Soviet Tower of Babel and could not complain from there, nor even appeal to the Soviet authorities. I was a nobody; I had been crossed out and I no longer existed. If they spit in my face, I had no right to be indignant. I had to wipe my face and remain silent. Only then could I hope to survive."

Davidoff has not reached the point in his healing process where he can go backward and forward in time with an inner sense of the continuity of life. "I had a feeling that I would be able to start life again, but later I found that was an illusion. During therapy, I understood the volume of all these hidden feelings and memories. They weren't something I could forget about and something that I could put somewhere very far away. They affected my thoughts and my emotions at a very close level of consciousness.

"All these memories, they create a problem. One is the feeling of guilt, similar to those in the concentration camps felt."

Davidoff survived torture by psychic numbing and cessation of feeling. Although he has made progress in reducing the number of flashbacks, he still lives in a world that neither lives nor moves. "I'm kind of frozen in this situation. I don't feel progress. I don't know why the process [of healing] is so sluggish. There's a feeling of loneliness about these memories. I write to get rid of them. There's no one person I could tell about what I felt, what I experienced and what I saw. It's impossible."

Shortly after his imprisonment, Davidoff refused to let the authorities cut his hair. He didn't think that he was committing a serious offense, but he was bound, beaten and led to a procedure room where a nurse cheerfully filled two syringes. "After these two injections, in 15 minutes, I was already more dead than alive. With great difficulty I managed to drag my mattress to the cell, threw it under the table and fell on it." He had no strength to cover himself with a blanket, and so he lay there half naked in the cold.

The next day a police van came to take him to the hospital. He lay inside the van on a bench, and every time they hit a bump in the road his bones ached painfully. When he arrived at the hospital, he was led through a building and a courtyard, then into an underground passage. When he entered the hospital ward, the prisoners were returning from a walk. "I was terribly frightened when I saw their faces. They were walking toward me, they were peering at me; I, the newly arrived prisoner, was the object of their interest. I noticed the old rags of their pajamas, their cleanly shaven heads, their restrained movements, their sunken cheeks, and, most frightening, their sunken eyes. Their eyes focused on one spot, clung to it and couldn't seem to shift in either direction. I will remember that frozen look to the end of my days. I thought, 'Will I become like them?' And I did."

The first days in the prison were the most terrifying, because he could still evaluate what was happening to him. "You understand that you are no longer in control of your body, no longer in control of your thinking, that you have ceased to think, that you are losing the ability to remember, losing everything you had—your hopes, your interests, your future, your memories. And gradually you reach the stage where all you can think of is your next meal. Gradually a person with high ideals becomes an animal who resides in the semi-underground cell of the Special Hospital, moves from side to side on his bunk, and exists from one piece of bread to the next."

On November 21, 1980, after two months in the Kazan psychiatric prison, he was led into a train. No one at Kazan explained anything to Davidoff, but a friendly convoy told him his file said "Blagoveshchensk," in the Soviet Far East, not far from the Chinese border. Davidoff rode in a cage with four other prisoners who argued about what they'd be getting for New Year's dinner—an apple or an orange.

When they finally arrived after a month and a half, the guards escorted them past a stone wall and Davidoff saw two slogans: "The health of everyone is everyone's wealth," and "Work is the first and natural necessity of human life." He remembered the slogan on the gates of Dachau: "Arbeit macht frei"—"Work sets you free." Although this message conveyed the notion that prisoners who worked would be freed, this proved to be a bitter lie. Davidoff was led upstairs, and although he had prepared himself for the worst, he was not prepared for what he saw. There were rows of cells on both sides of a long arched corridor. Some cells had no doors and were separated by thick metal bars and others were closed with a metal door that had only a small opening through which food was passed. A fine metal net covered the windows so the cells were dark. Naked light bulbs hung down from a cord from the ceiling. Rows of bunk beds stood close together but there were no stools or tables.

Prisoners moved in file along the only passageway. Agitated by the psychotropic drugs they were given, they paced several steps forward and then back again; others lay on bunks with their heads covered by thin blankets even though it was daytime. One inmate stared at Davidoff with glassy, indifferent eyes.

Two orderlies in black smocks and boots told the new arrivals to get dressed in what seemed to be a pile of rags.

"I got a pair of short trousers that came up to my knees and a light satin jacket with cut sleeves and torn pockets, and thin, prickly underwear. Instead of shoes, I was given big slippers, a size three times bigger than my own. My head was shaved although I only had half an inch of hair."

The prisoners were then taken to the quarantine cell where there were two beds for eight people. Cracks in the glass created a fierce draft and the glass itself was covered by frost that was an inch thick. "When I was kicked into that cell I felt very dizzy, tired and hungry. I began to tremble. I wanted to find a spot beside the barely warm radiator to warm up, but suddenly I felt water on my head and face. Water had condensed on the ceiling and drops were falling on me. When I realized I couldn't sit in that warm place, everything was so horrible. The next moment I experienced some kind of strange feeling. Suddenly, I felt that everything around me was happening, but not to me. Like it was not me there—not me, myself or I. I could only watch from a distant point. I lost the ability to feel anything. I didn't feel cold or tired. It was a strange experience. I was completely numb."

The feeling Davidoff describes of watching himself from a distant point is the process of disassociation. As a means of protection, people split off parts of themselves from awareness.

"On that day so many awful things had happened. I knew I would spend many years in this prison, although I didn't know how many. I was thinking two, three, five more years of this and it will be impossible to survive. I don't know what would have happened to these thoughts if I didn't get numb, finally and completely, when I felt those drops on my head."

As part of his recovery process, Davidoff has analyzed various aspects of what he suffered. "The worst situation was the drugs. I can separate their effects into three levels. On one level was the feelings which were active all the time, mostly physical symptoms: weakness, gasping. Also, there were moments I felt like I was dying because I couldn't get enough air. My heart was beating fast and irregularly. Then there was the second level, the mental level. When I tried to say something, very often I'd pronounce the first word or the second and forget what I wanted to say. I couldn't catch the thought and bring it back. It was real madness.

"There was also a third level of fear. It was like driving 90 miles per hour and approaching a downgrade. There's no time for reflection. It is all so uncontrollable and indescribable.

"I remember once I was awake and I was going from one wall to another. Maybe I didn't know what time it was, but I did know where I was. Then, bang. I found myself on the bed and didn't know how long I was there. It may have been only a few minutes but it felt like four hours. It was condensed time." Davidoff also remembered passing through some nightmares. "One was that I felt I was on fire. I looked at a small spot on my arm, and it began to grow and became black, yellow and red. When the whole spot became red, I saw that it was fire that was growing from inside my body. The whole feeling was fear and there was no time to think, 'Is this real or not?' I was always afraid they'd tie me to the bed and start drug injections. One time a prisoner punched a nurse and broke her nose. He was tied to a bed for 12 days and given repeated injections. Afterwards he couldn't get up. When I was watching this, I had a feeling that I was lucky.

"I remember once they beat my cellmate. Two big guards came in and beat this 17-year-old prisoner, who was tiny, for smoking in his cell; I couldn't do anything. If I had made a move to protect him, which I would have done had I not been in prison, they would have tied me to the bed and injected me, so I didn't do anything. They would have put me in the Special Treatment Cell with the most crazy prisoners, the ones who were frequently violent. So, you see there was a kind of hierarchy in a psychiatric hospital, and you could always move a step below. My situation was far from being the worst. Some people were getting stronger drugs, and since everyone was getting some drugs, I didn't feel totally alone."

Davidoff says that he survived by watching the people around him and learning from their experience. By learning how the system worked, he managed to stay out of trouble. "You see, I was from a different subculture. I had been a student, and I didn't know about life in prison. You were in a small cell with other people for 23 hours a day. If you got into a conflict, it could grow and become a nightmare. Some people committed suicide because someone in the cell with them was making life impossible."

In a secret message from his wife, who had poked pinholes in the pages of a newspaper, Davidoff learned about a campaign by Amnesty International to win his release. The psychiatrists at Blagoveshchensk began to treat Davidoff differently. He was allowed to keep a pen in his possession and was permitted to receive *Science and Religion* magazine.

During his second year of incarceration he managed to get "a foul book," *The Amusing Bible* by Leo Taksil. He crossed out all of Taksil's thoughts and read it like a Bible. He felt that he was on the border between life and insanity and felt a voice call to him, a spiritual voice from above. He watched many people who, when free, had been concerned with worldly things like money, drinking and cards, turning the cruel prison environment into divine power. "In that situation, a human being understood that he would not have sufficient strength to withstand the frightening effect of the perfected punitive machine, drugs. The only support, the only salvation, could be divine power, the power of the Savior."

During 50-minute walks in the courtyard, Davidoff and his friend Nikolai Borodin, who had regained his memory in spite of a course of injections, discussed religious subjects. "Nikolai had a good memory and had memorized texts. He knew the New Testament by heart. He quoted and quoted and quoted, and we discussed, argued at times and tried to penetrate the meaning of these Biblical words."

The talks with Nikolai had great meaning for Davidoff both because of their content and because of Nikolai's courage and stamina. Davidoff wondered what power enabled Nikolai to restore his abilities. Davidoff was amazed at how Nikolai "put together, bit by bit, his mental faculties" and was able to resist the pressure from the doctors to express remorse and renounce his faith.

In the spring of 1983, Davidoff found a copy of *Russkaya Mysl'*, published in Paris, which had been brought to a meeting at the hospital. Davidoff covered it with an issue of another newspaper and went to the courtyard and read every line. He told an interviewer for *The Samizdat Bulletin* that, "Suddenly I felt that I somehow managed to escape from that space-time dimension...that I was already a free man.... I felt that the walls had suddenly disappeared and I was out of the USSR, because that free style of expressing thoughts—thoughts that were not hindered as a force of habit, as is often the case with people who have lived in the Soviet Union—was an enormous space of fresh air which entered my lungs. I felt that I was ready to take off in flight."

After three years and eight months in Soviet psychiatric prisons, Davidoff was released. He worked as a night watchman, but did not sever contacts with his dissident friends. Soviet authorities suggested he emigrate. Since his marriage had ended while he was confined and he knew he wouldn't be able to stop his dissident activities, in April 1984, he left behind his parents, his friends and his country. The International Rescue Committee funded his trip from Vienna to the United States.

Davidoff's healing is still in process. He still has intrusive recollections of the trauma, a feeling of detachment from others and guilt about surviving when others didn't. However, through therapy, he has come alive in many of the ways in which he was previously dead.

He plans to study mysticism and, through knowledge of this dimension, to discover some ultimate meaning for his suffering.

Afterword

An extreme trauma does not end with the actual experience itself. If people are going to pull through the trauma, they need to regroup and make sense of what happened to them, to integrate the event into the lives they still have, but lives that are changed forever. Although extreme trauma can be very painful and sometimes life-threatening, adjusting to the new life after a catastrophe is usually a slow and gradual process, one that often requires a lifetime of dedicated and consistent work.

The stories just depicted describe the experiences of a selected group of people who suffered a horrific loss that severely threatened both mind and spirit. Despite the pain caused by the catastrophe, each person struggled, persevered and resisted defeat. And not only was each able to survive an unspeakably awful event, but they also discovered meaning and purpose in their tragedies; in different ways, the trauma redirected their thinking, opened up new roads, new skills, new priorities and new visions of the world and their place in it. Eventually, these positive elements helped these survivors emerge not only intact, but stronger and bigger than they were before the catastrophe. In this sense, without denying or forgetting the emotional wound, they all managed to cope and emerge victorious.

Recovery is no easy task and there are many people who are so ravished by experiencing a catastrophe that they are never able to retrieve a bearable life, one that is not weighed down forever by miserable emotional complications. The predictable world that they used to believe in and the tenets they used to live by — their very safety nets — were ripped away: there one minute, gone the next. Some trauma sufferers have repeated flashbacks and nightmares; others suffer terrible fear and are plagued by terror and helplessness. Some allow their emotions to flood out, and others respond with the total opposite — near amnesia with constricted, or no, feeling. These are the trauma survivors' attempts to find a balance with which they can comprehend and exist in an abruptly new life situation. A sense of balance, however, is exactly what a person who has just gone through a crisis usually does *not* have. When a horrible experience happens, especially when it comes with no warning, it shatters a person's sense that the world is a safe place that is made up of good people — and this is precisely what happened to almost every person in this book. That how "good" people are, or how careful they are *does not factor* into whether bad things can happen to them is, understandably, a terrifying realization. It can cause feelings of fear and intense alienation from others and the world itself. Like those I met in the emergency room, many come to see suicide as an effective escape from a sometimes hard and mean world.

The desire people have to end their lives seems to stem, in part, from the feeling that the world as they once knew it has been destroyed and that the trust and hope they used to have have been taken away forever. When the locus of control rules in circumstances that are external, one feels helpless, overwhelmed and frightened. As theologian Richard Niebuhr noted, "Suffering is a boundary of existence where our world appears to us as a field of energies converging on us, shaping us, distending us, shattering us and sending us on paths we have not chosen." That trauma usually — and understandably — extracts such an enormous psychological toll from its prey is precisely what makes the stories in this book so remarkable, so inspiring.

Indeed, among the most compelling aspects of these stories are the coping methods the survivors used, their processes of recovery and the ultimate transformation each achieved, despite how profoundly their world had been shattered. Although all the survivors coped with their particular crisis in their own way, they all used a few common methods. A fundamental part of this is the need to *reorient, embrace* and *integrate* the loss into their lives. They had to turn into the skid, so to speak, in order to keep from crashing; each of the people we have met in this book did this in some form or other. The process of integrating the trauma into their lives forced them to reassess their losses, priorities and values, which in turn required that each reexperience the catastrophe and to endure the pain, discomfort and frustration that accompanies this exploration.

These survivors used some of the following methods to work through their grief, to find a new vision that helped them transform themselves in a positive way:

1. They accepted what they could not change and they attempted to change what they could.
2. They acknowledged that there is a force or being greater than themselves and aligned themselves with this force. In other words, they saw themselves as part of a larger story that allowed them to feel more connected to, or more a part of, a larger universe. I hesitate to use the concept of religion because it is often shaped into strange forms by those who need a rigid belief system. So, using the definition that a religious person is someone who sees her life as part of a greater whole, a cosmic setting in which she plays just a part, many of the participants in this book became religious in a way they hadn't been before the catastrophe. Some felt that they became connected to spiritual forces; some called it mysticism; others fate; and still others God.
3. All of them went through such an awful ordeal that had they immediately faced the whole catastrophe head on, they probably would have burned out in no time. Many used some form of denial to compartmentalize the event. It is possible that, for some, this coping mech mechanism prevented a total breakdown. Recovery is

a slow, step-by-step process in which one must move from one stepping stone to the next in order to cross the river and reach the other shore. Gaining various things — the development (or retrieval) of self-esteem, for example — gave them the strength to face and, in turn, deal with the trauma in a more open way. Max Cleland illustrates this attitude well. Initially, after losing his legs, he was determined to walk again with the aid of prosthetic legs, despite what anyone said. He simply refused to believe that he would never walk again. He spent enormous energy learning to walk on the artificial limbs, interpreting the intense pain they caused him as a further test of his endurance. Eventually, he made successful strides in politics and this provided him with self-confidence. This self-confidence was the strength he needed to realize that he didn't have to use the artificial legs. Upon reaching this conclusion, he began using a wheelchair, and with the exception of special events, he never used the artificial legs again. He slowly found ways to face facts.

4. They realized that life *has* to be understood as an existence that includes hostile elements — malevolent others, accidents, illness and death. Direct and forced contact with these dark parts of life mobilized them to find a life that consisted of more than tragedy. The crisis made them ask questions about the fundamental safety and predictability of life, and what Albert Einstein said was the most critical question about life: "Is the universe a friendly place?" They had to realize that, just as people are constructed of both good and bad qualities, so too is the world in which we live. All found ways of understanding life that did not *eradicate* life's negative side, but instead *incorporated* it.

5. Many used some form of creativity to work through their grief. Creativity comes from deep within a person. For many, it helped because it made them face their anguish by incorporating pain with the joy of bringing something new to life, such as a piece of writing or art. By engaging in the creative process, they revisited and confronted their trauma, which in turn helped

them to find a new and more harmonious understanding that life is made up of extreme goods and
bads.

6. Several of these survivors used writing as a way to
cope; it helped them to recapitulate and reconstruct
the trauma. Through poetry, Armando Valladares
found horizons that could not be barb-wired. Elie
Wiesel's novels chart a positive movement from angst
to an affirmation that there is life beyond despair.
This helped him to explore abysses in human nature
that defy easy understanding. In his books, Wiesel uses
metaphors to unite the opposing aspects of existence
and creates conversations between his characters to
resolve his own inner struggles. Through a creative
process, many were able to transform their psychic
wounds into something positive. If someone is gifted
or has a spark of genius, the creative product of his
mourning may be a great work of science or art. Although the trauma *did not create* the person's gifted-
ness, it provided the creative energy. The way the
anguish of loss can ignite passion is well illustrated
by the screaming horse in Picasso's painting *Guernica*.
Guernica expresses Picasso's outrage at the bombing of
a helpless town by fascists during the Spanish Civil
War. In stark blacks and grays, the figures are torn
apart, their faces distorted. In this painting, Picasso
illustrates how art can unite opposites and, because
understanding this is a fundamental part of recovery,
why it can be a useful way to work through grief.

7. Many of them healed themselves by helping others. In
that tender realm in which one who has been hurt can
help someone who is hurting, they healed themselves.
After the impotence they felt following the catastrophe,
they uncovered a sense of power by offering strength
to others. Rabbi Harold Kushner found himself in a
most difficult situation after his son died. Here was a
man who preached that devoted faith to God was a
path toward redemption. Then suddenly, his omni-
scient God did not prevent his son from dying. How
could he continue on with the same beliefs he had

before when suddenly the God he had such strong
faith in abandoned him in his time of need. This is a
good example of how *anything* can suddenly happen
to *anyone* at *anytime*. Everything the man believed in
— and even preached to others — the very ground
upon which he so faithfully stood — suddenly caved
in right before his eyes and he felt angry and betrayed.
But Kushner found a way to conquer this feeling, in
part by realizing that God does not cause events to
happen, but that he *is* here to help us get through the
chaos that is so characteristic of life so we do not feel
alone in our suffering. As well, Kushner healed by
finding that he was uniquely qualified to help others
and this was his stepping stone to gaining back his
strength. All of the survivors learned that "looking out
for number one" is only useless expenditure of
negative energy.

8. When threatened by anger or bitterness, they eventually
realized it only made them hurt more and made a conscious effort not to be consumed by it. As one of Elie
Wiesel's characters says,"What matters is not to give
up...not to become resigned or bitter. Bitterness is the
worst of all evils." Anne Capute also knew she had to
let go of the anger she felt toward the many people
who turned on her when she was facing a murder
charge. After his son died, Richard Herrmann began
searching for lessons of love and forgiveness because
he could not stand the idea of being an angry and
bitter man for the rest of his life.

9. They focused on hopeful visions of the future, not on
what they could no longer do or have. For some, the
determination to overcome adversity became the
cornerstone of a new identity, some describing an
almost mystical rebirth. Erik Erikson believed that
there is a connection between hope and religion, that
hope is the first, most important and indispensable
virtue inherent in the state of being alive."If life is to
be sustained, hope must remain even when confidence
is wounded and trust impaired." Erikson believed that
what begins as hope in the infant becomes in its mature

form, faith.

10. They became motivated to achieve a symbolic form of immortality by living on through living more moral lives. Mike Wallace redirected his life and changed his entire attitude toward life by making a commitment to become the kind of person his son would have admired.

This list is not meant as a set of rules for all people who have suffered severe trauma. To really know something is to dwell in it, to restructure it in your own terms and metaphors. If you are trying to recover from a trauma, how you respond depends entirely on the specific tragedy you face and the kind of person you are. What worked for Andre Dubus, Rabbi Kushner, or Mike Wallace may not work for you. The list shows only what a select group of people did.

I want the reader to understand that I deliberately chose to interview people who had suffered extreme trauma and who had exceptional coping skills. I did this so that you can meet role models who might inspire you. Additionally, the losses they experienced are very extreme, but again, this was a deliberate choice on my part because I want you to see that the resilience they called upon can be used by others who have experienced less catastrophic losses. In other words, if you, the reader, are suffering from a trauma — perhaps the loss of your marriage or the loss of your job — the coping methods these survivors used can be helpful to you. The stories describe the paths that these people followed and, more important, they demonstrate that not only *rejuvenation*, but also that *transformation* of the soul following catastrophe is indeed obtainable.

Although these survivors fought hard against being overwhelmed by different crises — a disabling disease, unjust imprisonment, war injuries — all of them discovered that interconnection with others was a critical part of their healing. They came to realize that we are all part of a human community in which we need each other. As noted earlier Alcoholics Anonymous and Narcotics Anonymous also stress the acknowledgment of a higher being, a force greater than themselves and members also dedicate themselves to helping others learn how it is possible to overcome problems.

Finally, why would well-known people be willing to share their deepest and most painful experiences with me and, in turn, with you? We tell our stories, no matter how horrible, so others can be there with us, see what we saw, hear what we heard, and feel what we felt. It is widely believed that such communion is at the heart of healing.

Sometimes the process of converting raw recall into a narrative enables people to understand their experiences in a new way. Also, reexperiencing the trauma before an attentive listener often leads the teller to a different, sometimes more ojective angle from which they can view themselves. And reviewing the past, present and future enables them to incorporate losses into the whole fabric of their lives in a more comprehensive way. Listening to another person's story cannot help but enlarge ones sense of humanity.

To those who may be trying to incorporate a trauma into their lives, I hope these survivors' stories will make you feel less alone. As Martin Buber said, "When a man is singing and cannot lift his voice, another sings with him, another who can lift his voice so that the first will be able to lift his voice, too. That is the secret bond between spirits." Buber believed that all healing takes place in an exchange of hearts. I hope that meeting the remarkable people whose stories are told in this book — people who struggled through the abysses of human existence — will enlarge you and will help soothe your passage through difficult times.